Psychotherapy
with Homosexuals

CLINICAL INSIGHTS

INNOVATIONS IN

Psychotherapy with Homosexuals

Edited by
EMERY S. HETRICK, M.D.

Clinical Assistant Professor of Psychiatry, New York University—Bellevue Medical Center; and Institute for the Protection of Lesbian and Gay Youth, Inc., New York

TERRY S. STEIN, M.D.

Associate Professor and Director of Medical Student Programs in Psychiatry, Department of Psychiatry, College of Human Medicine and College of Osteopathic Medicine, Michigan State University, East Lansing

AMERICAN PSYCHIATRIC PRESS, INC.
Washington, D.C.

© 1984 American Psychiatric Association

Library of Congress Cataloging in Publication Data

Main entry under title:

Innovations in psychotherapy with homosexuals.

  (Clinical insights)
  Half title: Psychotherapy with homosexuals.
  Includes bibliographies.
  1. Homosexuality.   2. Psychotherapy.   3. Hetrick, Emery S.,
1930–   .   II. Stein, Terry S., 1945–   .   III. Title: Psychotherapy with
homosexuals.   IV. Series. [DNLM: 1. Homosexuality.   2. Homosexuality,
Ego-Dystonic—therapy.   3. Psychotherapy.   WM 615 I58]
RC558.I56   1984   616.85′83406   84-14485
ISBN 0-88048-055-6 (pbk.)

Printed in the U.S.A.

Contents

Contributors

CAROL J. COHEN, M.D.
Private Practice, Berkeley, California

EMERY S. HETRICK, M.D.
Clinical Assistant Professor of Psychiatry, New York University—Bellevue Medical Center; and Institute for the Protection of Lesbian and Gay Youth, Inc., New York

JAMES P. KRAJESKI, M.D.
Private Practice, San Francisco

A. DAMIEN MARTIN, Ed.D.
Associate Professor, School of Education, Department of Communication Arts and Sciences, New York University, New York; and Director of Education, Institute for the Protection of Lesbian and Gay Youth, Inc., New York

ANDREW M. MATTISON, M.S.W., Ph.D.
Assistant Clinical Professor of Family Medicine, University of California at San Diego, School of Medicine; and Private Practice, The Clinical Institute of Human Relationships, San Diego

DAVID P. MCWHIRTER, M.D.
Assistant Clinical Professor of Psychiatry, University of California at San Diego, School of Medicine; and Private Practice, The Clinical Institute of Human Relationships, San Diego

SALLYANN ROTH, M.S.W.
Private Practice; Co-Director, The Family Institute of Cambridge; Lecturer in Psychology, Department of Psychiatry Harvard Medical School, Boston, Massachusetts; and Lecturer, Smith College School of Social Work, Northampton, Massachusetts

TERRY S. STEIN, M.D.
Associate Professor and Director of Medical Student Programs in Psychiatry, Department of Psychiatry, College of Human Medicine and College of Osteopathic Medicine, Michigan State University, East Lansing

Introduction

The medicalization of sex was well under way by 1869 when a somewhat obscure Swiss physician, Karoly Maria Benkert, coined the term *homosexual*. Medical study and classification of sexual behavior seemed to be an advance, especially for those classified as deviant. A homosexual male, described only as a highly placed British official, sent the following to Krafft-Ebing:

> Your opinion that the phenomenon under consideration is primarily due to a congenital 'pathological' disposition will perhaps make it possible to overcome existing prejudices and awaken pity for poor, 'abnormal' men, instead of the present repugnance and contempt. Much as I believe that the opinion expressed by you is extremely *beneficial* [sic] to us, I am still compelled, in interest of science, to repudiate the word 'pathological.'. . .According to my firm conviction, by far the greater number of cases of mental disturbance or abnormal disposition observed in homosexuals are not to be attributed to the sexual anomaly; but they are caused by the existing notions concerning homosexuals, and the resulting laws, and dominant public sentiment concerning the anomaly. Any one with an adequate idea of the mental and moral suffering, of the anxiety and care that the homosexual must endure; of the constant hypocrisy and secrecy he must practice in order to conceal his inner instinct . . . can only be

We would like to thank Professor A. Damien Martin and Ms. Jan Baer for their criticisms, suggestions, and help with this manuscript.

surprised that more insanity and nervous disturbance does not occur in homosexuals.

With the shift to a sickness model, causes had to be found and treatments devised. Two major causes were proposed: homosexuality as an atavism and homosexuality as inhibited or pathological development. The former, championed by Krafft-Ebing among others, was soon dropped in favor of the latter, of which psychoanalytic formulations are the best known. Treatment consisted of a wide variety of techniques, many of which are quite reminiscent of today's behavioral modification. Most of the early clinicians, however, concluded that it was not possible to change the basic orientation, although the patient could sometimes learn to function sexually with the opposite sex. In this sense so-called modern approaches are not innovations but merely a replication of earlier nineteenth century approaches that have been proven failures (see Chapter 2).

The collection of papers in this monograph represents a major innovation in the treatment of the homosexually oriented. The innovation does not lie so much in the originality of the concepts—Karl Ulrichs proposed a theory of homosexuality as a normal variant of human sexual behavior in 1862. Indeed, the model of ego-dystonic homosexuality offered by Hetrick and Martin in this volume is prefigured by the "highly placed British official" quoted above. Rather, the innovation lies in the shift from a sickness model to one that holds homosexuality to be a normal sexual variant for purposes of treatment. This change in treatment focus is a logical result of the 1973 modification of the Diagnostic and Statistical Manual in which homosexuality was dropped as a diagnostic category.

The chapters in this monograph address a variety of issues pertaining to the clinical treatment of gay and lesbian people. While gay and lesbian people can develop psychiatric conditions suffered by those with heterosexual orientation, the authors of this monograph do not address questions of differential diagnostics. Their attention goes to the first order of business after the psychiatrist is freed from the concept of homosexuality itself as the illness: how can the therapeutic process deal with the problems that result from systemic negative attitudes about gay and lesbian people?

Emery S. Hetrick, M.D.

References

von Krafft-Ebing R: Psychopathia Sexualis: With Especial Reference to the Antipathetic Sexual Instinct. Translated from the 12th German edition by Klaf F. New York, Bell Publishing Co, 1965

1

Ego-Dystonic Homosexuality: A Developmental View

Emery S. Hetrick, M.D.
A. Damien Martin, Ed.D.

1

Ego-Dystonic Homosexuality: A Developmental View

In 1973, the American Psychiatric Association removed homosexuality from its list of disorders. In 1980, The Diagnostic and Statistical Manual, third edition, (DSM-III) included as one of its categories the term "ego-dystonic homosexuality." Based on a phenomenological and descriptive approach, the diagnosis depends on meeting the following criteria: A. the individual complains that heterosexual arousal is persistently absent or weak and significantly interferes with initiating or maintaining wanted heterosexual relationships; B. there is a sustained pattern of homosexual arousal that the individual explicitly states has been unwanted and a persistent source of distress (DSM-III 1980).

The essential factor is the individual's adverse reaction to his or her homosexual orientation. Without this adverse reaction, a sustained pattern of homosexual arousal and an absence or weakness of heterosexual arousal that interferes with initiating or maintaining heterosexual relationships merely describes a homosexual sexual orientation. A heterosexual orientation might also be described as a sustained pattern of heterosexual arousal and the absence or weakness of homosexual arousal that interferes with maintaining homosexual relationships. The critical distinctions in the diagnosis of ego-dystonic homosexuality, therefore, are the negative reaction to and desire to change one's sexual orientation.

This chapter will not address the controversy surrounding either the appropriateness of the term itself or the inclusion of the category in the DSM-III (Bayer and Spitzer 1982). Rather, it will propose a theoretical and clinical perspective within which the phenomenological criteria should be interpreted. This perspective suggests that the criteria, as described, are consistent with societally induced developmental stages through which most homosexually oriented people must pass before achieving full emotional maturity as self-accepting individuals. That is, within the social and psychological context of social identity as a homosexual, unhappiness at having a homosexual orientation and desire to have heterosexual relationships are normal and to be expected at some stage of an individual's development.

This is not to say, however, that some individuals do not need help in dealing with these stages. Indeed, in the more severe cases, ego-dystonic homosexuality may represent an arrest at a specific stage of social and personal development with a concomitant intensification of self hatred that necessitates professional help. In additional instances, ego-dystonic homosexuality may also exist as part of a wider disturbance. In all cases, however, including the most severe, the phenomenological criteria are derived from problems with personal and social identity rather than sexual orientation per se.

It will be further suggested that some current treatment approaches (Masters and Johnson 1979; Pattison and Pattison 1980; Kaplan 1982) may possibly exacerbate the etiological components in the phenomenological criteria specified for ego-dystonic homosexuality, thus intensifying both their pathogenic and stress-inducing possibilities.

IDENTITY

Identity is a broad category that is usually divided into two separate but related subcategories or areas: *personal identity* and *social identity*. Personal identity can be defined both as the sense of one's ongoing uniqueness as an individual and the intrapsychic processes that support that sense. On the other hand, social identity in the broadest sense refers to a socially defined role within either a group or category of persons. Traditionally, psychiatry and psychology have claimed the areas of personal identity while sociology and anthropology have focused on social identity. Although sometimes reified, both forms of identity are abstractions rather than concrete states, and both are concepts built upon perceptions and characteristics that shift according to context. For example, social identity as a priest, with the concomitant demands made upon behavior, will be different when the individual is in the company of other priests or members of his parish or when he may be in mufti and enjoying a party with lay friends. The personal identity of an individual who is a priest will depend on a number of other historical and social factors that interact with the individual's own awareness and perception of the self developed through time. Social identity relates more to the society's expectations of the individual in his or her role, whereas personal identity is usually discussed in terms pertaining to intrapsychic processes.

In all disciplines, concepts of identity usually include the formulation of movement or development toward the identity. Social identity in an occupation, for example, may involve stages of preparation as well as maturation within the identity. Similarly, personal identity may be described within the framework of developmental stages through which one moves rather than as an actual given state (Freud 1905; Erikson 1963). At any stage the person may be caught in conflict. Even gender identity, which would seem to be concrete, depends on processes of maturation and acculturation.

Although personal and social identity are separated conceptually, the two categories are linked in that the individual's personal and intrapsychic identity often depends in large part on the demands and expectations that make up one or more of his or her social identities.

Interaction of Personal and Social Identity

Ideally, personal and social identities interact in mutually supportive ways, enabling the individual to cope with life's vicissitudes to the best of his or her personal capacity. The impact of a social identity on a sense of self, especially on the developing sense of self, depends in part on the range and implications of the category for both the individual and society. A social identity as a Jew will have a different impact on the developing personal identity of the Jewish individual depending on whether or not he or she is living in an antisemitic society, a comparatively neutral society such as the United States, or a positively reinforcing society such as Israel.

When a social identity carries a stigma, the impact on personal identity can be especially strong. Stigmatization, as a communicative and social process, has as its purpose the negating of the group and individual members of that group. As Goffman puts it in his aptly titled work *Stigma: Management of Spoiled Identity*,

> By definition, of course, we believe the person with a stigma is not quite human. On this assumption we exercise varieties of discrimination, through which we effectively, if often unthinkingly, reduce his life chances. We construct a stigma-theory, an ideology to explain his inferiority and account for the danger he represents. . . . Further, we may perceive his defensive response to his situation as a direct expression of his defect and then see both defect and response as just retribution for something he or his parents or his tribe did, and hence a justification of the way we treat him. (Goffman 1963, 5–6)

Sexual orientation is both a social and a personal identity. It is personal because it is innate within the individual, and it is social because society uses this identity for assignment of prescriptive normative rules that must be learned and conformed to within the socialization process. Sexual orientation has far-reaching social, religious, and legal implications within our society with concomitant effects on the individuals concerned.

For the heterosexually oriented, the implications of sexual orientation as a social identity are generally positive; one is constantly reinforced for being heterosexual. A homosexual sexual orientation, however, generally brings a host of sanctions by society that, as Goffman described, denotes the orientation as defect and castigates the individual for the defensive response.

These sanctions in turn inculcate negative reactions in the homo-sexually oriented.

For both the heterosexually and the homosexually oriented, however, the ideal interaction between personal and social identity within the context of sexual orientation could be defined operationally as a functional integration of sexuality and emotionality (Troiden 1979). A number of factors may interfere with the development of this integration for both the heterosexually and the homosexually oriented. Difficulties may result from such factors as religious teaching about sexuality in general, social customs limiting social and sexual interactions, fixed and rigid gender roles, personality disorders, and depressions. For the homo-sexually oriented, however, the major difficulty comes from the totality of the social stigmatization directed against them.

Stigmatization of the Homosexually Oriented

One's reputation, whether false or true, cannot be hammered, ham-mered, hammered, into one's head without doing something to one's character. A child who finds himself rejected and attacked on all sides is not likely to develop dignity and poise as his outstanding traits. On the contrary, he develops defenses. Like a dwarf in a world of menacing giants, he cannot fight on equal terms. He is forced to listen to their derision and laughter and submit to their abuse. ... His natural self love may under the persistent blows of contempt, turn his spirit to cringing and self hate. (Allport 1958, 138–139)

According to Allport (1958), a minority group is any group that suffers from unjustifed negative actions by the dominant group. Within the framework of this definition, gay people qualify for minority status (Martin 1982a).

In common with other minority groups, gay people may develop a number of coping mechanisms or strategies which, while largely intrapsychic and personal, derive from and are inextricably linked with social identity. The emotional and psychological distress resulting from the conflict between homo-sexual desire and internalized prohibitions can range in severity from mild and transient discomfort to severely crippling guilt and shame anxiety. Indeed, in the "coming out" process most if not all gay and lesbian people experience some degree of discomfort in reaction to which they employ one or several overlapping coping stratagems. Allport (1958, 139-157) describes 15 such "ego defenses" that develop because of the victimization of minority group members by the dominant group. His descriptive categories of coping have application to gay and lesbian experience. Stratagems include such devices as denial of membership in the hated group, obsessive concern with social role, identification with the dominant group, self hate, and aggression against one's own group. Of the 15 defenses listed by Allport, two are particularly relevant to this discussion and can provide additional understanding about the relationship between symptoms brought by the individual to the treatment setting and the social attitudes informing those symptoms.

Because the deep and basic insecurity about acceptance by others can pervade relationships as the gay person is coming out, the easiest defense to employ is simply to deny to oneself and to others that one is a member of a hated group (Martin 1982a). The denial frequently takes the form expressed by the phrase, "This is not part of me—just a phase" (Troiden 1979). Denial of membership does not merely eschew involvement or participation but also insistently denies that any characteristic of the hated group has any positive value. The second relevant coping strategy is identification with the dominant group. Here the individual turns the introjected anger and revulsion against the self into the production of shame and guilt. In turn, this supports the persistent demand that the self extirpate the unwanted homosexual desire, nourish heterosexual urges, and change the orientation.

One additional identity problem should be noted. A minority group member may believe that anything unwanted or unpleasant is always related to the particular stigma. For example, a black may come to believe that anything negative that occurs in life comes from his being black. Similarly, the gay or lesbian person may come to believe that most personal difficulties are related in some way to his or her homosexuality. A corollary holds that a change in sexual orientation or sexual behavior will bring happiness and the resolution of most conflicts (Pattison and Pattison 1980). Since each of the above defenses is engendered in part by societally supported stigmatization processes, each may be considered symptomatic of a societally induced condition. Parenthetically, let it be noted here that this is where treatment approaches directed toward inducing or encouraging heterosexual behavior in the individual with ego-dystonic homosexuality may harm through exacerbation of these negative and unrealistic views.

The stigmatization process is the same for any group and consists of three stages: *antilocutions*, the negative verbal treatment of the group; *discrimination*, the differential treatment of the group based on group membership; and finally, *violence* against the group. All minority groups suffer from societal actions at all three stages (Allport 1958).

The actual actions taken against the minority group at any stage will differ depending on the nature of the group and the antecedent societal actions against the group. For example, although both antisemitism and racism were prevalent in the United States, economic and social discrimination against Jews was never as powerful as that directed against blacks.

Gay people differ from other minority groups in one way essential to the development of integrated and thus mutually supportive personal and social identities. Most members of other minority groups are born into their groups and are raised within the social structure of that group. Even under the most terrible economic and social deprivation, the black, the Jew, or the gypsy can at least develop that most essential characteristic of group and social identity, the sense of "we" versus "they" (Allport 1958). Gay people usually enter their group during adolescence. (We speak here of the beginning of personal and social identity as a gay person rather than the beginning of sexual orientation per se. Evidence indicates that the latter occurs much earlier than adolescence.) Dank (1971) pinpointed this difference when he wrote the following:

> ... in the sense of early childhood socialization [the homosexual minority is not like the negro minority] for the parents of a negro can

communicate to their child that he is a negro and what it is like to be a negro, but the parents of a person who is to become homosexual [sic] do not prepare their child to be homosexual—they are not homosexual themselves, and they do not communicate to him what it is like to be a homosexual.

This late acquisition of social identity as a homosexually oriented person has several important implications.

First, unlike members of other minority groups, gay or lesbian people have no preparation for their social identity. They often lack appropriate or correct information about homosexuality and its management. For example, the young person often has been exposed only to misinformation and absurdities about gay people, including charges that the homosexually oriented have destroyed civilizations (Buchanan 1977), cannot whistle (Ellis 1936), lack body hair (Decter 1980), caused the Second World War and the American defeat in Vietnam (Podhoretz 1977), are child molesters who commit the most corrupt and heinous of sins (Smith and Dilenno 1979), betray our mammalian heritage and are all unhappy (Socarides 1975, 1978), and cannot form mature nonerotic friendships with either sex (Pattison and Pattison 1980). Usually, little opportunity exists for the young person to find out the truth about even these most extreme views.

Even more damaging, the young gay or lesbian adolescent has no opportunity to learn the social management of sexuality in a positive manner. Nongay adolescents have role models and instruction for both courtship procedures and social responsibilities in sexual relationships; the young gay male or lesbian has none (Martin 1982a). As a result, young gay males, in particular, may rely solely on sexual activity as a means of making contact within their group, at least until they reach the age when they can enter the primary structure for begining socialization of the gay person, the gay bar (Roesler and Deisher 1972).

The problems imposed by restrictions on nonsexual support systems is not, however, limited to adolescence for gay and lesbian people. American society has done all in its power to prevent the formation of alternative social structures that could provide nonsexual, community-based support for the homosexually oriented.

In 1964, Congress passed a bill, HR5990, forbidding the granting of nonprofit status to a homophile organization that engaged in educational and charitable work. As recently as 1983, the Attorney General of the state of Mississippi refused nonprofit status to the Parents and Friends of Lesbians and Gays, Mississippi, Inc. and the Mississippi Gay Alliance, Inc., on the grounds that approving a nonprofit charter ". . .would ostensibly give official legal status to an organization dedicated on its face to subverting this statute." (*Washington Blade*, December 9, 1983, 5). (The statute in question reads as follows: "Every person who shall be convicted of the detestable and abominable crime against nature committed with mankind or with a beast, shall be punished by the imprisonment in a penitentiary for a term of not more than ten years.")

Exactly the same reasoning was used in 1970 by the Secretary of State of New York to deny incorporation status to a homophile organization. That decision was unanimously reversed by the Appelate Division of the New York Supreme Court (*Gay Activists Alliance v. Lomenzo* [1971]; *Owles v. Lomenzo* [1972]).

Second, a lack of perceived congruence between other social identities for which the child has been trained and social identity as a homosexual leads to cognitive dissonance (Festinger 1957). Cognitive dissonance can only prevent the development of that ego-identity that Erikson (1963, 261) defined as

> [t]he accrued confidence that the inner sameness and continuity prepared in the past are matched by the sameness and continuity of one's meanings for others.

For example, a child raised in a religiously orthodox family may have emotional and psychological difficulties reconciling religious and sexual identities. Thus although Weinberg and Williams did not find significant differences according to religion in their cross-cultural study of male homosexuals, they did find that

> [r]espondents who attribute the most importance to religion are more worried about exposure of their homosexuality, more concerned with passing, and less known about than homosexuals for whom religion is not important at all. In addition, respondents who personally evaluate

religion as important are more likely to define other people's opinions as important to them, suggesting that religious respondents are more other directed. (Weinberg and Williams 1974, 253)

To use Erikson's terms again, the "inner sameness" and the "sameness . . . of one's meanings for others" were discongruent, with expected results. Weinberg and Williams also found that

> [h]olding religiosity constant . . . among those who regard religion as very important, those who perceive homosexuality as more in violation of religion score lower in stability of self-concept (and in the United States, self acceptance) and higher in depression than do those who do not perceive such a violation. We find no significant relationships among those who do not regard religion as very important. (255)

In other words, self acceptance, stability of self concept, and even presence of depressive symptomatology, were found to depend on interrelationships with the prescriptive social norms of other social identities rather than on the presence of a homosexual orientation.

Third, stigmatization of the homosexually oriented demands that the individual hide his or her sexual orientation. Although the pressure to "remain in the closet" continues through the lives of most gay people, it appears initially in adolescence. At a time when heterosexual adolescents are learning how to socialize, young gay people are learning to conceal large areas of their lives from family and friends. As a result, most relationships, particularly familial relationships, become based on deception (Martin 1982a). The ever present need to self monitor and the reinforcement this gives to lowered self esteem and a sense of worthlessness was summarized for other conditions by Perry et al. (1956):

> The awareness of inferiority means that one is unable to keep out of consciousness the formulation of some chronic feeling of the worst sort of insecurity, and that means that one suffers anxiety and perhaps even something worse . . . the fear that others can disrespect a person because of something he shows means that he is always insecure in his contact with other people; . . . now that represents an almost fatal deficiency of the self system.

It is only to be expected that gay and lesbian people would want at some point in their lives to escape the pressures described above, to wish that they were not homosexually oriented, and even to desire heterosexual relations. The majority of gay people, however, although often suffering through such a turbulent phase, eventually do develop mature, mutually supportive personal and social identities as homosexually oriented persons (Bell and Weinberg 1978; Bell et al. 1981). This goal is reached, however, only after the gay individual has learned to cope in a positive manner with the differences between an intrapsychic and personal identity based on negative, and usually incorrect, societal expectations about homosexuality and the homosexually oriented, and an actual identity based on personal experience and relationships with other gay people.

Troiden (1979) proposed a preliminary model of the stages one must traverse to reach the ideal fusion of personal and social sexual identity that we will call a *gay identity*. He interviewed 150 white gay men between the ages of 20 and 40. From their responses he identified four stages involved in reaching a gay identity: *sensitization, dissociation* and *signification, coming out,* and finally *commitment*. For our discussion, stages two and three, *dissociation* and *signification* and *coming out,* are the most important, for it is during these stages that characteristics typical of ego-dystonic homosexuality occur.

Dissociation and Signification.   In this phase the individual is aware of the presence of homosexual feelings and actions. In many the feelings are dissociated and the acting out behavior denied as being part of the personality. By denial and dissociation the individual attempts to exclude portions of awareness that would be indicative of belonging to and participating in a hated subgroup. Yet the act of denying signifies the degree of implicit importance these feelings and behaviors have for the nascently gay individual. Troiden quotes as characteristic such phrases as "passing through a phase," "curiosity," "something I would outgrow," and "mere experimentation." At the risk of being obvious, these forms of denial all utilize a basic tenet of psychodynamically based theories of homosexuality as a developmentally centered phenomenon.

The dissociation described by Troiden is basically the same phenomenon described above by Allport as often occurring in minority groups: denial of group membership and identification with the dominant group. It would appear that the two criteria for a diagnosis of ego-dystonic homosexuality, unwanted homosexual arousal coupled with a wish for heterosexual arousal, are a reflection of societally induced states associated with stigmatization and have little or nothing to do with sexual orientation.

Coming Out. To escape from the conflict laden stage of dissociation, it is necessary for the individual to progress to the next stage, coming out. This stage has three sequential components: self identification as having a homosexual sexual orientation, initial contacts with the gay subculture, and redefinition of homosexuality as being part of a viable lifestyle.

> I knew there were homosexuals, queers and what not; I had read some books, and I was resigned to the fact that I was a foul, dirty person, but I wasn't actually calling myself a homosexual yet. . . . I really caught myself coming out [when] I walked into this bar and saw a whole crowd of groovy, groovy guys. And I said to myself, there was the realization, that not all gay men are dirty old men or idiots, silly queens, but there are some just normal looking and acting people, as far as I could see. I saw gay society and I said, Wow, I'm home" . . . that night in the bar. I think it saved my sanity. I'm sure it saved my sanity. (cited in Dank 1971)

The first two components, self identification as a homosexual and initial contacts with the gay subculture, usually have a positive long-term impact, and they result, in time, in the third component of the coming out process, redefinition of homosexuality as a viable life style. The achievement of this redefinition is essential to the final stage of achieving a gay identity, the integration of sexuality and emotionality.

In some cases of ego-dystonic homosexuality, however, self identification as having a homosexual orientation and contact with the gay subculture may intensify the conflicts. The former may mean self identification as defective while the latter, because of the nature of most initial contacts, may exacerbate feelings of failure and rejection. For example, the subjects in Pattison and Pattison (1980) state that their unacceptable homosexual sexual orientation rendered them immature, unhappy, and incapable of mature, nonerotic friendships with men and women. Accordingly, to reach emotional maturity, to have nonerotic friendships, and to achieve happiness, they must follow their church's teaching and change to a heterosexual orientation. For these men, self identification as homosexual signaled self identification as defective in their religion and as human beings incapable of interacting with others in a meaningful way.

This feeling of alienation from other homosexuals may be exacerbated by the nature of initial contacts with the gay subculture. In spite of recent changes, the bar continues to be the major social institution that provides a nondangerous meeting place for the younger person, particularly the male, until integration into the subculture allows the individual to develop a network. Since the legal age for drinking in most states remains at 21, initial involvement in the gay subculture may be only sexual in nature, devoid of other dimensions (Roesler and Deisher 1972; Martin 1982a). The young male may then continue to compartmentalize his sexual behavior separate from other noneroticized affectional and social interactions. This compartmentalization may either prevent the young male from using the nonsexual social possibilities in the subculture or lead him to believe on a subliminal level that sexual success is concomitant with group membership. Failure to succeed may then be equated with failure to be accepted by the group. Thus, questions about the use of sexuality may become confused with issues surrounding orientation itself, further inhibiting the orderly development of integrated sexuality and emotionality.

Intensification of social isolation and self loathing through failures in social interaction are not unique to the homosexually oriented, of course. Nevertheless, when Jews in an antisemitic society encounter these problems, neither they nor their therapists ordinarily think that a change in religion would resolve the issues. Similarly, if a black person were to come to a therapist demeaning his or her race, the therapist would not encourage the use of hair straighteners and skin bleaching creams as a solution to their ego-dystonic reaction to their race. Nor is there any indication that a change in sexual orientation would help the inhibited sexual desire of the heterosexual (Kaplan 1983). At the risk of being obvious, the reason such therapy is not offered is because hetero-sexuality, and the heterosexually oriented, are not stigmatized in our society. Although obvious, the point is worth stressing.

The important question is, what type of treatment, if any, is appropriate for those ego-dystonic individuals who suffer from self hate, obsessive concern with social identity, identification with the dominant group that promulgates the negative self image, who deny membership in the hated group, and may even perform acts of aggression against their own group?

Implications for Treatment

Denial of group membership and identification with the domi-nant group by the labeling of homosexual desire as unwanted and heterosexual desire as more acceptable are two coping maneuvers often used in attempts to deal with a stigmatizing social identity. The distress arising from belonging to a stigmatized minority can range from normal identity conflict to pathological levels of despair and depression. Criteria for undertaking therapy and type of intervention should be based on the severity of the reaction as well as other factors. In some cases assistance might lie in providing the individual with accurate information about homo-sexuality and the gay community, giving an introduction to resources including self-help groups within the gay and lesbian community, or perhaps guiding the person to gay socialization groups. In the more severe cases, reduction of the distress may take the form of more conventional therapy. Therapies that purport to treat ego-dystonic homosexuality either through changing sexual orientation or "expanding the sexual options" of the individual should either be avoided completely or approached with great care and skepticism. Space does not permit a detailed examination of these therapies at this time, but a few points should be made. Chapter 2 examines them in greater detail.

The belief that the homosexual orientation itself is the cause of the psychological and emotional distress—a belief shared by the ego-dystonic homosexual as well as by many clinicians—is an example of the *post hoc, ergo propter hoc* fallacy in logic. That is, since the homosexual orientation precedes the distress, the distress must stem from the homosexual orientation. Historically, this fallacy has led to the treatment of the gay person through trying to change his or her sexual orientation. Even those therapists and treatment approaches that do not have change as the overt goal, who speak instead of "expanding sexual options," implicitly support the belief by the patient that the origin of the presenting problems is homosexuality rather than the internalized negative societal attitudes that result in self-hatred. It is frequently stated— and believed—that achievement of heterosexual behavior, especially marriage, will not only signal change in sexual orientation but also eliminate unhappiness. One homosexual cited in Bell and Weinberg's *Homosexualities* said,

> It's [homosexuality] lonely. Marriage and children are guarantees against loneliness. Although I've made up for this, in part, by being a teacher, I still regret not having had my own children. (Bell and Weinberg 1978, 123)

While no one should object to the expansion of sexual options, the meaningful limits of such expansion must be recognized, both by the patient and the therapist. Much of the available evidence suggests that ignoring these limits can have disastrous results for the individual, especially when unrealistic expectations about change, and the role that marriage will play in such change, are a factor in the individual's desire for treatment (Cory 1951; Dank 1972; Westwood 1960). Freund (1977, 238–239), with an openness not often found in most writings on therapy, wrote the following:

> Almost 20 years ago I started a therapeutic experiment, employing aversion therapy combined with positive conditioning toward fe-

males. Approximately 20 percent of the homosexual males, who came of their own accord to ask for help, married and founded families. For some time there seemed to be reason for guarded optimism. However, this was a long-term study, and these marriages were followed up for many years. Virtually not one "cure" remained a cure. The patients had become able to enjoy sexual intercourse with females as well, though much less than with males, but there was no true, lasting change in sexual preference. . . . Many victims admitted this only much later than they themselves had clearly noted the fact. . . . I am not happy about my therapeutic experiment which, if it has "helped" at all, has helped clients to enter into marriages that later became unbearable or almost unbearable. Virtually all the marriages of these clients had become beset with grave problems ensuing from their homosexuality.

Even when only one of the goals of therapy is expansion of sexual options, it must be made clear that this may not solve many of the patient's difficulties. Just as heterosexually oriented persons may experience homosexual arousal under certain conditions, so too may the homosexually oriented experience heterosexual arousal. In neither case does this signal a change in libidinal direction for object choice. This must be made clear to the individual undergoing treatment. The clinician as well as the patient must realize that sexual behavior of any kind will not solve the identity problems faced by the individual. Therapy must be directed toward acceptance of one's sexual orientation. The patient as well as the therapist must understand that the goal should be the integration of sexuality and emotionality, not just the performance of a specific sexual act.

CONCLUSIONS AND SUMMARY

A rationale for diagnosis should include the answers to three questions: What is the nature of normal functioning? What is the nature of the disorder? And finally, what etiological factors may bring about the disorder?

In establishing the diagnosis of ego-dystonic homosexuality, the DSM-III does not develop answers to these questions. This chapter has attempted to offer a framework within which they can be addressed. We have suggested that concepts of normal functioning must include the development of mutually supportive social and personal identities as a foundation for the integration of sexuality and emotionality. The successful integration of these two areas is essential for the acquisition of a positive gay identity. We have further suggested that the disorder now called "ego-dystonic homosexuality" is an expected stage in that development and as such can be considered a disorder only to the degree to which it interferes with further development toward the ideal integration of sexuality and emotionality. And finally, we have suggested that the etiology of both the normal stage of unease with a homosexual orientation as well as dissatisfactions that more clearly need professional intervention result from society's stigmatization of the homosexually oriented.

Problems with the development of a mature sexual identity are not limited to homosexuals; heterosexuals can often have difficulty achieving integration of sexuality and emotionality. These problems, however, are not seen within the historical or individual context of attempts to change sexual orientation. Although we have not addressed the issue of ego-dystonic homosexuality versus ego-dystonic heterosexuality, the concept of developmental stages leading to a mature sexual identity suggests that a more appropriate category might be ego-dystonic sexuality.

Finally, we touched on issues having to do with treatment. Although various treatment approaches were not examined in detail here, we did suggest that treatment of patients for ego-dystonic homosexuality without understanding the social and psychological dynamics involved in society's stigmatization carries risk of doing harm to the patient. If marriage is presented as an option, that harm may be generalized to the family. Consideration of these possibilities becomes an ethical as well as professional responsibility.

References

Allport G: The Nature of Prejudice. Garden City, NY, Doubleday, 1958

Bayer R, Spitzer RL: Edited correspondence on the status of homosexuality in DSM-III. J Hist Behav Sci 18:32–52, 1982

Bell A, Hammersmith SK, Weinberg MS: Sexual Preference: Its Development in Men and Women. Bloomington, Indiana University Press, 1981

Bell AP, Weinberg MS: Homosexualities: a Study of Diversity among Men and Women. New York, Simon and Schuster, 1978

Buchanan P: Gay day: Looking beyond the Miami mauve movement. *New York Daily News*, June 7, 1977

Cory DW: The Homosexual in America: A Cross-Cultural Approach. New York, Greenberg, 1951

Dank BM: Coming out in the gay world. Psychiatry 34:180–197, 1971

Dank BM: Why homosexuals marry women. Medical Aspects of Human Sexuality 6:14, 1972

Decter M: The boys on the beach. Commentary 70:35–48, 1980

Deisher R, Roesler T: Youthful male homosexuality. JAMA 219:1018–1023, 1972

Dilenno JA, Smith HJ: Sexual Inversion, The Questions: The Church's Answers. Boston, Daughers of St. Paul, 1979

Ellis H: Sexual inversion. From Studies in the Psychology of Sex, abstract 891. New York, Random House, 1936

Festinger L: A Theory of Cognitive Dissonance. Evanston, Ill., Row, Peterson, 1957

Freud S: Three essays on sexuality, in The Standard Edition of the Complete Psychological Works of Sigmund Freud, vol. 7. Translated and edited by Strachey J. London, Hogarth Press, 1953

Freund K: Die Homosexualist, 2nd ed. Leipzig, S. Hirzel, 1965

Freund K: Should homosexuality arouse therapeutic concerns. J Homosex 2:235–240, 1977

Gay Activists Alliance v. Lomenzo, 66 Misc, 2d 456 NY Supp 2d 994, 1971

Goffman E: Stigma: Notes on the Management of Spoiled Identity. Englewood Cliffs, NJ, Prentice Hall, 1963

Kaplan HS: ISD: A model for the treatment of ego-dystonic homosexuality. Presented at Conference on Homosexuality: A Decade of Development. New York, March 1982

Martin AD: Learning to hide: the socialization of the gay adolescent. Adolesc Psychiatry 10:52–65, 1982a

Martin AD: The minority question. etcetera 39:22–42, 1982b

Masters WH, Johnson VE: Homosexuality in Perspective. Boston, Little Brown and Co, 1979

Owles v. Lomenzo, 38 App. Div., 2d 981 NY Supp 2d 181, 1972

Pattison EM, Pattison ML: Ex-gays: religiously mediated change in homosexuals. Am J Psychiatry 137:1553–1562, 1980

Perry HS, Gawell M, Gibbon M: Clinical Studies in Psychiatry. New York, WW Norton, 1956

Podhoretz N: The culture of appeasement. Harpers, October 1977, pp 25–32

Schwartz MF: The Masters and Johnson approach to the treatment of ego-dystonic homosexuality. Presented at Conference on Homosexuality: A Decade of Development. New York, March 1982

Socarides C: Beyond Sexual Freedom. New York, Quadrangle, 1975

Socarides C: Homosexuality. New York, Jason Aronson, 1978

Troiden RR: Becoming homosexual: a model of gay identity acquisition. Psychiatry 42:362–373, 1979

Weinberg M, Williams C: Male Homosexuals. New York, Oxford University Press, 1974

Westwood G: A minority: A Report on the Life of the Male Homosexual in Great Britain. London, Longman, 1960

The Emperor's New Clothes: Modern Attempts to Change Sexual Orientation

A. Damien Martin, Ed.D.

2

The Emperor's New Clothes: Modern Attempts to Change Sexual Orientation

According to the well-known saying that hunger and love rule the world, quackery has from its earliest beginnings concerned itself by preference with the provinces of disorders of digestion and of sexual troubles; and especially in respect of the latter have its developments been so astounding. In fact there appears to be nothing else which gives such instructive information regarding the possibilities of human folly, depravity, and superstition. (Bloch 1908, 721)

Case 48. Reported by Dr. Wetterstand. Cultivated Contrary Sexual Instinct Cured in Three Weeks by Suggestive Treatment. . . . Patient has a stately figure, is masculine in his whole appearance and physically well formed. In a week he was transformed by treatment. Coitus was successful. I can definitely assert that when he left he was entirely cured, and that after treatment for about three weeks. . . . He is about to marry. (von Schrenk-Notzing 1892, 221)

R . . . did convert [to heterosexuality]. He began functioning successfully in intercourse on the tenth day of therapy. (Masters and Johnson 1979, 353)

INTRODUCTION

Prior to the nineteenth century, the subject of homosexuality was primarily the domain of the theologian. The advent of the enlightenment in the seventeenth century, however, had signalled an end to theology's monopoly on the discussion of sex, and scientific investigation of sexual behavior, including homosexual behavior, became a possibility. Nevertheless, old attitudes die hard and the still prevalent religious tradition of antisexuality created an atmosphere in which only the physician could study sex. As late as 1896, John Addington Symonds complained that discussion of homosexuality was

... peculiarly difficult, and exposes the enquirer, unless he be a professed expert in diseases of the mind and nervous centres, to almost certain misconstruction. (5)

Although an advance from theology's restrictions, the medicalization of homosexuality was not without its disadvantages. The physician's professional imperative to diagnose and treat often combined with his personal, religious, and ethical beliefs to create a situation where religious premises were offered as scientific support for both the supposed illness and treatment of the homosexual.

Despite the conversion of religious belief into diagnostic and treatment entities, the introduction of scientific method had a long-term beneficial effect. Unlike western theology, science demands that its basic assumptions be constantly questioned and reevaluated in light of the evidence. One such evaluation process resulted in the 1973 decision by the American Psychiatric Association (APA) to remove homosexuality from its list of mental disorders (Bayer 1981). With this action, the APA caught up with Freud who, in 1915, added the following footnote to his seminal "Three Essays on a Theory of Sexuality":

Psychoanalytic research is most decidedly opposed to any attempt at separating homosexuals off from the rest of mankind as a group of special character. (1905, 145)

In 1980, the APA's *Diagnostic and Statistical Manual of Mental Disorders* (3rd ed.) included a new diagnosis, "ego-dystonic homosexuality," in which (1) the individual complains that heterosexual arousal is persistently absent or weak and significantly interferes with initiating or maintaining wanted heterosexual relationships, and (2) there is a sustained pattern of homosexual arousal that the individual explicitly states has been unwanted and a persistent source of distress.

At least three possible causes for the ego-dystonic distress can be posited: (1) homosexuality itself, in which case ego-dystonic homosexuality becomes a sexual disorder; (2) psychiatric illness that is at least concomitant if not causal; or (3) factors like stigmatizing socialization that are only tangentially related to sexual orientation.

If homosexuality itself were the root cause of the distress, one would logically expect the majority if not all of the homosexually oriented to be ego-dystonic. Researchers from von Krafft Ebing (1896) to Weinberg and Williams (1974) have repeatedly reported, however, that most gay people are happy and satisfied with their sexual orientation, chafing only under society's stigmatization.[1] (Notes appear after the reference list.) The relation of ego-dystonic reactions in the homosexual to other psychiatric conditions, especially depression, has been relatively unexplored. The importance of such a possible relation lies not just in the causal role that psychiatric illness may play in the ego-dystonic phenomena, but in an evaluation of the possible effects of various therapies. For example, the Masters and Johnson Institute program excludes only subjects who have a history of psychosis, alcoholism, or drug addiction (Schwartz and Masters 1984), ignoring the possible effects of their therapy on borderline individuals and those with bipolar illness or other psychiatric conditions.

A more logical answer to the question of etiology lies in the third possibility, specifically the development of ego-dystonic phenomena as a result of the minority group status of gay people (Chapter 1) (Martin 1982a, 1982b; Goffman 1963; Allport 1958). Accordingly, it would seem to follow that therapy should attend to the internalized self-hatred of the ego-dystonic homosexual rather than his or her sexual orientation per se. Three major therapeutic approaches proposed in recent years (Masters and Johnson 1979; Pattison and Pattison 1980; Kaplan 1982) do not take that direction, choosing instead to follow the traditional approach of attempting to change sexual orientation.

This chapter offers a critical examination of these three approaches. Many of the issues raised also apply to other change-oriented therapies, especially psychoanalytic approaches. Reference will be made to other therapeutic attempts to change sexual orientation, but space limitations do not allow for an extensive historical review of this literature despite its obvious relevance.

The "Ex-gay" Movement

"I know what you're thinking about," said Tweedledum; "but it isn't so nohow."
"Contrariwise," continued Tweedledee, "if it was so, it might be; and if it were so, it would be; but as it isn't, it ain't. That's logic."
(Lewis Carroll, *Through the Looking Glass*)

In all persons I have observed, they first became Christians, began to develop a pattern of spiritual growth within which they came to view homosexuality as unacceptable and sinful, and as a result of their spiritual growth changed their sexual orientation. (Pattison 1977, 107)

The "ex-gay" approach might seem inappropriate to a discussion of therapy since it centers around religious practice and belief. Nevertheless, it is germane to this discussion for five reasons. First, religion has played a major role in the development of rationales and methods for treatment (Moore 1945; Vanderveldt and Odenwald 1957) and in the development of negative attitudes toward homosexuality and thus in the development of ego-dystonic homosexuality (Greenberg 1973; Hellman et al. 1981; Larsen et al. 1983) (see also Chapter 1). For example, Weinberg and Williams (1974) found that when compared to other male homosexuals, those homosexuals who rated religion as very important and who viewed homosexuality as sinful had a lower self-concept and were more depressed, worried about exposure, concerned with passing, and apprehensive about other people's opinion of them. Yet, despite the apparent importance of religious attitudes to negative social and intrapsychic attitudes and thus to the development of ego-dystonic homosexuality, little research has been attempted in this area.

Second, the ex-gay movement is offered and advertised as a form of therapy. Third, the publication of a descriptive paper by Pattison and Pattison in the *American Journal of Psychiatry* (1980) has given the movement professional respectability as a therapeutic approach. Fourth, the principles upon which it is premised are supported and promulgated by mental health professionals (Morris 1978; Pattison and Pattison 1980). For example, William P. Wilson, the Head of the Division of Biological Psychiatry at Duke University Medical Center, wrote the following:

> Treatment using dynamic individual psychotherapy, group therapy, aversion therapy, or psychotherapy with an integration of Christian principles will produce object choice reorientation and successful heterosexual relationships in a high percentage of persons. . . . Homosexuals can change their sexual orientation. God has condemned homosexual behavior and has made the power to change available to those who desire it. Therefore, "homosexual and Christian" is a contradiction. Homosexuals have no excuse, but if they desire change, they do have hope. (Wilson 1979, 167)

And finally, although exact figures are not available, the number of ego-dystonic homosexuals seeking help in the "ex-gay movement" far exceeds those seeking help from more professionally acceptable sources. For example, one group, the Exit Ministry, reported 300 individuals seeking help over a five-year period (Pattison and Pattison 1980), while Masters and Johnson (1979) treated only 67 over 10 years and Helen Singer Kaplan (1982) has reported on only two cases.

Religious experience and consequent changes in attitude and behavior are valid, heuristic areas for study by the behavioral scientist. Religious belief as either clinical rationale or therapeutic tool, however, does not vitiate the need for the scientist to observe the same care and skepticism he or she would use in evaluating any clinical research.[2]

Pattison and Pattison (1980, 1559) claim to have produced the "first documented study (excluding single anecdotes) of profound behavior and intrapsychic change in sexual orientation from exclusive homosexuality to exclusive heterosexuality without long term psychotherapy" through the use of Christian principles and practice. To reach this conclusion, they reviewed one church group's records. Over a five-year period, 300 individuals who were unhappy with their sexual orientation had sought help. Of that 300, only 30 (10 percent) claimed to have changed from homosexuality to heterosexuality. Of the 30, only 11 agreed to take part in the study. Pattison and Pattison do not discuss the refusal to participate by the other 19 "cures."

Perhaps the first point to stress is that Pattison and Pattison's conclusions are based on 3.6 percent of a total population. An additional point of interest about the study population is that eight of the 11 subjects cluster in all categories: eight subjects report an almost euphoric state (1556); eight subjects have no neurotic symptoms; eight subjects agree on the cause of their homosexuality (1558); eight subjects are rated as "cured" (1560); and, crucial to an appreciation of the data, eight were actually working for the crisis center. The Pattisons offer no discussion of this remarkably consistent pattern.

While inconsistencies between the tables and the body of the text, inaccurate and misleading statistics, and factual errors in the reporting of data from other studies make the study difficult to discuss (Hetrick and Martin 1981), the major problems revolve around investigator bias, the description and discussion of the therapeutic approach, and the validity of the supposed results. Accordingly, the following discussion will focus on these three areas.

Investigator Bias. Scientists and clinicians always approach their investigations with some degree of subjective feeling, even if those feelings are only expectations arising from commitment to a theoretical model. The objective scientist, completely rational and above the influences of personal opinion and feeling, is a myth. Therefore, a given in research design is the provision of some measure of reliability and validity in data collection and interpretation. The inclusion of safeguards is especially important when an investigator has strong personal feelings about either the subject matter or the subjects.

In an earlier paper (Pattison 1974, 343), the senior author suggested that heterosexuals "with secure identity will usually experience disgust toward homosexual acts" and that any heterosexual who did not feel such disgust suffered from a failure in "psychosexual identity development." Pattison qualifies this by asserting that " . . . we distinguish between the acts of a person and the person." The posture is an extension of the religious stance that one must love the sinner while hating the sin. Since it is impossible to treat the sin/illness without treating the sinner/patient, the distinction appears meaningless. Additionally, since all sexual acts performed by homosexuals are also performed by heterosexuals, the inference must be that Pattison, whether intentionally or not, is speaking of homosexuality and homosexuals.

Everyone, of course, has a right to have a personal reaction, even one of disgust. But this explicitly negative reaction becomes important when, as in the study discussed here, the only claims for the reliability and validity of the data rest on the Pattisons' personal feelings:

> Although the subjects knew we were investigating their changes in sexual orientation, we do not believe that this substantially [sic] biased the data; they were forthright about the personal details of their past and present life and did not attempt to distort their life experience . . . even though much of the subject material related to issues of considerable shame, guilt, and anguish to the subjects. (Pattison and Pattison 1980, 1554)

and on the following:

> . . . a set of corollary data that confirmed the subjects' claims that they had changed in sexual orientation was obtained from the staff of the crisis program, and from the spouses of the six subjects who were married. (1554)

The corollary data are not given. No explanation is offered as to how interviews with the staff, who were coworkers, fellow religionists, and cosubjects could substantiate the heterosexuality of the subjects, especially since five of the 11 were not performing

sexually in any manner. Nor is any indication given of an attempt
to allow for the response bias expected from religious homosexuals
who are highly sensitive to the opinions of others (Weinberg and
Williams 1974) and who were speaking of a subject that produced
within them "considerable shame, guilt, and anguish."

Therapeutic Regime.   The closest the study comes to specify-
ing a theoretical rationale for the therapy is in this statement:

> Within the Church's ideology was the explicit assumption that
> homosexuality was a maturational deficit that resulted in an inability
> to engage in mature non-erotic love with both men and women. As a
> result of maturing in appropriate interpersonal relations, a man was
> expected to develop an erotic attraction to a woman as a mature love
> object. Sexual experience then would follow appropriately within
> marriage. (1556)

This rationale is not discussed to any great extent. Nor do the
authors explain how the two subjects who had married and
experienced heterosexual intercourse before their "maturation"
would fit into the Church's ideology. The interesting aspect of the
rationale lies in its couching of a secular theory in religious terms.
The developmental anomaly theory espoused by the Church is
fundamentally a restatement of a nineteenth century construct of
Social Darwinism, derived in part from the now rejected "ontog-
eny recapitulates phylogeny" hypothesis (Sulloway 1979).[3]

The therapy derived from this evolutionary cum theological
rationale apparently consists of religious study and witness, group
pressure, and group support. The group, described as "a guiding,
sustaining, and *disciplining* Christian community" (Pattison
1977) [emphasis added] tries to guide the homosexual to a "commitment" to Christ and the Church. Such commitment is defined
as the prerequisite for emotional and social maturity and thus to a
renunciation of homosexuality and growth into heterosexuality.

Group pressure and support are widely used therapeutic techniques. One would have hoped, therefore, for an extended discussion of the group's strategies and interactions, but no such discussion is offered. Indeed, although contradicted by the internal
evidence of the text, pressure is denied.

When our subjects came in contact with the Church's crisis service for homosexuals, they found a welcome reception as homosexuals. No attempt was made to change their homosexuality. (1558)

The evidence of the text contradicts this claim: " . . . subjects were exposed to an ideological expectancy set demanding growth in personal and interpersonal maturity" (1558) so that "as a result of maturing in appropriate interpersonal relations, a man was expected to develop an erotic attraction to a woman as a mature love object" (1556). These goals were explicitly political—"the term ex-gay had been deliberately selected by them to denote an ideological position in opposition to 'gay liberation' "—and the pressure to change is specified: The clients were "invited" to "commit their lives to Christ and the Church" while being taught that the Church " . . . defined heterosexuality as a necessary component" (1558). After "small church fellowship groups" had taught these men that the homosexual is psychologically immature and has poor interpersonal relationships, the subjects reported that they "soon became aware that they were psychologically immature and had poor interpersonal relationships" (1558).

Since therapy can be conceptualized as a form of pressure toward change, the denial of that pressure by the researchers might be nothing but a reportorial curiosity if the amount and type of pressure put on these subjects were not crucial to an understanding of the "clever Hans" effects so evident in the subjects' responses. This in turn is critical to an understanding of the claims for therapeutic success.

Therapeutic Results. Five of the married subjects presented "intrapsychic evidence of current homosexuality," including " . . . persistence of homosexual impulses [that] was still significant." Yet the marriage of six of the 11 subjects, two of whom had been married before their entry into the program, is presented as evidence for change. The authors explain this discrepancy by claiming that the married subjects are just like all other normal heterosexual males who occasionally have tinges of "homosexual ideation." In their conclusions, they ignore the "intrapsychic evidence" and "persistence of homosexual impulses" of these five subjects and claim that only three subjects do not "amply demonstrate a 'cure' " (1560).

Long before there were any therapies, Ulrichs (1868, 70), pointed out that most of the practicing homosexuals he knew were married. Moll (1897), Forel (1905), Krafft-Ebing (1896), von Schrenk-Notzing (1892), Ellis (1891), and a host of others warned that marriage was no indication of a change of orientation and often led to disastrous results for everyone concerned. One need not even go back to the nineteenth century. Several modern studies indicate that at least 20 percent of gay men have been married at least once (Bell and Weinberg 1978; Weinberg and Williams 1974; Saghir and Robins 1973; Curran and Parr 1957; Parr 1957) and that even in those cases, marriage by the homosexual may not have the same meaning that it has for the heterosexual. Perhaps most importantly, marriages that result from "therapy" are more likely to be unhappy (Freund 1977). Marriage is not an adequate indication of change of sexual orientation.

The evidence for change is even weaker for the unmarried subjects. Since the strictures of their religion forbid nonmarital sexual behavior of any kind, these subjects were completely celibate. The Pattisons reassure us, however, that " . . . all of them looked forward to marriage and three were actively dating" (Pattison and Pattison 1980, 1557). In other words, two putatively heterosexual subjects could not interact with the opposite sex on a simple social level like dating, and yet Pattison and Pattison provide us with the age at which they changed to heterosexuality and the length of time this change has persisted. Despite their own claim that "suppression of overt homosexual behavior or involvement in heterosexual activity does not constitute a 'cure' or change in sexual object choice" (1560), the authors offer both the celibacy of some subjects and the marriage of others as evidence for a change of sexual orientation.

The Pattisons' confusion between sexual behavior and sexual orientation is not unique. Feldman and MacCullough (1971) listed as "improved" those homosexual subjects who had ceased to perform sexually with other men but who could not yet bring themselves to date or kiss a woman. Feldman and MacCullough went even further than the Pattisons, however. They also rated as improved those homosexuals who decreased the variety of sexual acts indulged in with the same sex.

One result of this confusion between the sexual act and the sexual orientation is that all therapies to change sexual orientation report efficacy. Everything that has ever been tried—hydrotherapy, (Krafft-Ebing 1896, 1965) hypnosis (von Schrenk-Notzing 1895), shock treatment (Owensby 1940, 1941; Thompson 1949), a single interview (Berg and Allen 1958), psychoanalysis (Bieber et al. 1962), and correct breathing and biting towels (Kronemeyer 1980)—has been "successful" in changing the homosexual.

Homosexuals involved in the "ex-gay" movement do not themselves make the claims that Pattison and Pattison make for them. They often admit that their change consists of avoidance of homosexuality through membership in a Christian community[4] rather than any switch to heterosexuality (Boone 1978; Blair 1982; Philpott 1975, 1977). As one "ex-gay" put it,

> All I knew is [sic] that I didn't like the homosexual life style and I wanted out of it. I just thought of myself as a new creature in Christ, naturally part of the family of God. I was no longer a homosexual, but I did not consider myself heterosexual. Women still did not appeal to me. . . . And if I stay single the rest of my life, this is just fine with me, I'm happy the way I am. I don't need a wife, though I might like to have one. (Philpott 1977, 34)

Another member of the ex-gay movement said,

> Initially, when I first had my renewal experience, I hadn't resigned myself to give up sex. That happened a few months later as the Holy Spirit began to convict [sic] me. . . . Marriage isn't repulsive. It's just that I can't accept in my own mind emotionally, the sex act. You see any kind of sex act is repugnant to me right now. This is a terrible emotional burden that has to be resolved. (Philpott 1975, 76–77)

Although one may sympathize with the sense of comfort these men obtain from their religious identification, neither this comfort nor their celibacy can stand as a valid criterion of sexual orientation change.

The sense that a social identity as a homosexual precludes a social identity as a Christian seems to be both the central issue and overriding rationale in the ex-gay movement. Since being a homosexual and Christian at the same time is a "contradiction," the acquisition of a Christian identity will of necessity preclude a homosexual identity (Wilson 1979, 167; Gangel 1978; Morris 1978; LaHaye 1980; Pattison and Pattison 1980): " . . . they first became Christians . . . and as a result of their spiritual growth changed their sexual orientation" (Pattison 1977, 107). Unfortunately, it does not seem to work that way. A dropout from the "ex-gay" movement states,

> . . . we prayed and pleaded with God for deliverance from our homosexual nature. . . . Although I was completely open and honest before God, my homosexual feelings remained. . . . There are some gay Christians still claiming to be 'ex-gay' but these statements are being made by faith as they continue to suppress their homosexual feelings (Blair 1982, 7)

One final note: the two founders of "Exit," the program from which Pattison and Pattison obtained their subjects, including one who married, have since left the program and returned to male lovers (Blair 1982).

The Pattisons' claim to have documented a change of sexual orientation in these subjects cannot be accepted.

INHIBITED SEXUAL DESIRE

> "When I use a word," Humpty Dumpty said, in a rather scornful tone, "it means just what I choose it to mean—neither more nor less."
> "The question is," said Alice, "whether you *can* make words mean so many different things."
> "The question is," said Humpty Dumpty, "which is to be master—that's all." (Lewis Carroll, *Through the Looking Glass*)

Helen Singer Kaplan's approach to treating the ego-dystonic

homosexual, like the approach described by Pattison and Pattison, has the changing of the homosexual orientation as its aim. There can be little discussion of the therapy itself since she does not specify techniques, evaluative criteria, or follow-up procedures (Kaplan 1974, 1982). Her therapeutic approach to ego-dystonic homosexuality is apparently a combination of psychoanalytic insight therapy and behavior modification techniques. While she gives no citations, Kaplan's explication of ego-dystonic homosexuality as fear of the male and ambivalence toward women merely restates one traditional psychoanalytic theory that, like many psychoanalytic formulations, has no empirical base. Nor does Kaplan offer any evidence to support the concept. Perhaps the best discussions of this hypothesis can be found in Ferenczi (1916), Stekel (1922), and Kardiner (1954).

Although not specified by Kaplan, improvement in her therapy appears to be successful heterosexual coitus. There can be little doubt that behavior modification techniques can and do lead some ego-dystonic homosexual males to erection and heterosexual intercourse, but since situational heterosexuality—like situational homosexuality—is well reported in the literature, her reports of success are neither surprising nor important. Nevertheless, an examination of Kaplan's work is essential for two reasons: first, although she gives no evidence other than simple assertion to support her claimed success in treating ego-dystonic homosexuality, her claims have remained unchallenged; second, her therapeutic rationale is based on a hybrid diagnosis not found in DSM-III. This rationale and diagnosis contradict the stated position of the profession: that homosexuality is not of itself a mental disorder. The following discussion, then, will concentrate on her rationale for treatment of the ego-dystonic homosexual.

Situationally Inhibited Sexual Desire

Diagnosis and therapy always depend on clinical definitions of normal functioning, most of which fall into one of four epistemological constructs: normality as health, normality as utopia, normality as transactional systems, and normality as average (Offer et al. 1974). Kaplan borrows from all four but depends mainly on the last, the equation of the average with normal (Kaplan 1974, 1979, 1982, 1983).

Although she admits that reliable and valid norms do not exist, Kaplan feels they are unnecessary because of a "sufficient professional consensus . . . [and] enough of a sense of what the normal range of sexual interest is for practical purposes "(Kaplan 1979, 58–59). She neither references nor documents this consensus nor explains what "practical purposes" it serves.

Kaplan expands on her concept of consensus normality with a triphasic model of sexual functioning—(1) desire, (2) excitement, and (3) orgasm—in which impairments at any phase are "separate diseases" (1983, 8). Homosexuality, therefore, is a pathological deviation in the desire phase, because it involves "desire for an object or situation which does not interest the majority of persons" (1979, 64). In other words, heterosexual sexual behavior is the norm because that is what most people do; conversely, therefore, homosexual activity is pathological because most people are heterosexual. Carried to its logical extreme, Kaplan's definition automatically defines blue eyes, registration in a parochial school, or belief in and submission to psychoanalysis as pathological deviations from the norm.

Kaplan's designation of homosexuality as pathological immediately places her in conflict with the APA's position that homosexuality is not in and of itself a mental disorder (Bayer 1981). While disagreement is appropriate and necessary in matters so nebulous as "normal sexual functioning," a clinician has a professional and ethical obligation to specify the disagreement and to explain carefully why an opposing stand is taken. Kaplan does not affirm the difference except to make one unfortunate and misleading reference to what she designates as the "gay point of view" (Kaplan 1979, 64) and does not explain the rationale behind her disagreement except to say " . . . it makes more sense to me" (1983, 239). The view she characterizes as "gay" is held by the National Institute of Mental Health Task Force on Homosexuality, The American Psychiatric Association, The American Psychological Association, and numerous avowed heterosexual researchers.

After developing a model of normality from an admitted lack of data, Kaplan creates a new diagnosis, Situationally Inhibited Sexual Desire (SISD), which she describes as " . . . little or no desire in situations which most persons would find erotic, i.e., an intimate sexual relationship with an attractive partner of the opposite gender" (1979, 64). SISD is a seeming modification of an officially recognized diagnosis, Inhibited Sexual Desire (ISD), which is defined in DSM-III as persistent and pervasive inhibition of sexual desire. It is only a seeming modification because the central issue in ISD is specifically the question of intensity and frequency of sexual desire, while the central issue in Kaplan's SISD is the type of sexual desire.

ISD clearly has nothing to do with homosexuality. However, Kaplan's addition of the arbitrary term *situational* permits the inclusion of phenomena that have nothing to do with the diagnostic criteria in the original diagnosis, even when the intensity and frequency of sexual desire is within expected limits. The illogic and contradiction should be apparent. A homosexual who has frequent and intense desire for members of the same sex is by no stretch of the imagination suffering from an inhibition of sexual desire. Rather, the strong desire for a member of the same sex with a corresponding lack of desire for the opposite sex is merely a possible definition of homosexual desire, just as a strong desire for a member of the opposite sex with a correspondingly low desire for members of the same sex could define heterosexuality. Neither have anything to do with the original DSM-III concern with the intensity and frequency of desire.

The distortion occasioned by the non sequitur nature of SISD is not helped by Kaplan's reductionist argument that impaired sexual desire, homosexuality, fetishism, sadomasochism, bestiality, cross-dressing, and exhibitionism have

> . . . two essential components: low or absent desire for and gratification from sexual intercourse with a heterosexual partner in a committed and intimate relationship, with normal or intense desire and gratification in the variant situation. (1983, 239)

The justification is a meaningless tautology. It simply posits that three distinctly different conditions—impaired sexual desire, paraphilias, and ego-dystonic homosexuality—are the same because they differ from heterosexual behavior. A parallel argument would be to group Blacks, Catholics, and accountants as a single entity because they are not British.

Kaplan further defends her characterization of homosexuality as situationally inhibited desire by claiming that impaired sexual desire and ego-dystonic homosexuality respond to treatment techniques, including her own (1983, 8). Three objections to this nonsequitur come immediately to mind. First, the three studies she cites, Beiber et al. (1962), Feldman and MacCullough (1971), and Masters and Johnson (1979) are highly questionable as evidence for successful therapy.[5] Second, even if the claims for therapeutic success were true, they would not prove that homosexuality is pathological. Many left-handed people were forced to use their right hands; that does not prove that sinistrality is pathological. Third, the lack of published material on her treatment of the homosexually oriented prevents any evaluation of her claims for success and therefore renders such claims useless as evidence to support the diagnosis.

Kaplan's rationale for considering homosexuality as pathological within a framework of "Situationally Inhibited Sexual Desire" is both tautological and logically inconsistent. The lack of specification of her treatment procedures and criteria for evaluation of success or failure, the lack of detailed followup, and the lack of substantiation for her claims of therapeutic success raise the issues far beyond the success or failure of the putative therapy. Indeed, the more appropriate question may center around the appropriateness of this approach with disturbed people.

Masters and Johnson

> 'Twas brillig, and the slithy toves
> did gyre and gimble in the wabe:
> All mimsy were the borogoves,
> and the mome raths outgrabe.
> (Lewis Carroll, *Jaberwocky*)

There are multiple problems in Masters and Johnson's description of their attempts to change homosexuals into heterosexuals (1979). These problems include, but are not limited to, failure to review the appropriate literature; lack of a specified rationale; failure to report specific techniques or criteria for evaluation of those techniques, thus rendering replication impossible; failure to specify methods of follow-up; and contradictory statements, logical fallacies, and inconsistencies.[6] Space does not allow a detailed discussion of all these difficulties; therefore, the following will attend to only two of the many problems presented by the study: the unexamined negative attitude toward homosexuality that pervades the work, and the claim that their techniques have succeeded where other therapies have not.

Their negative attitude is important in the sense described above for Pattison and Pattison. The subjective beliefs and attitudes of clinicians and researchers cannot help but have an effect on therapy and the evaluation of its results. The only recourse for the clinician/researcher is to recognize and specify these negative attitudes and to try to find means to minimize their effects. Admittedly this is more difficult in therapies like this than it is, for example, with medical treatment of physical disease. Yet there is an obligation at least to try to keep the problem in the forefront of consciousness.

Masters and Johnson do not recognize the negative nature of their attitudes toward homosexuality. Indeed they emphasize their neutrality and lack of heterosexual bias (1979, 272). Nevertheless, despite disclaimers, their work regularly displays the heterosexual bias they so vigorously deny. Prejudicial comments like the suggestion that the phrase "it takes one to know one" serves as "a most effective homosexual recruiting slogan for the sexually timid" (212) might be dismissed as momentary lapses. More important are their clinical and theoretical biases as to how homosexuality develops and about the supposed "inherent long-range disadvantages" in long-term committed homosexual relationships.

According to Masters and Johnson, both heterosexuality and homosexuality are learned. Heterosexuality, however, is the natu-

ral result of a development without "psychosocial roadblocks."
Homosexuality, however, is the result of these "psychosocial
roadblocks to effective heterosexual interchange." Their examples, drawn from individual case histories, are exemplary illustra-
tions of the post hoc ergo propter hoc fallacy in logic; that is,
because one event precedes another event, it must be the cause. For
example, one of their patients supposedly became homosexual
because he had been ridiculed for poor performance in his
previous attempts at heterosexual behavior. The possibility that
his heterosexual performance might have been poor because he
was homosexually oriented is not raised by Masters and Johnson.
While redundant, it is appropriate to point out that this is another
instance of the unsupported developmental anomaly explanation
of homosexuality.

The purported "inherent long-term disadvantages" in homosexual relationships supposedly stem from what at first glance would
appear to be an advantage, the higher subjective involvement in
sexual interaction between homosexual couples. Masters and
Johnson explain that this advantage is only apparent because it
arises from "*necessity*" (their emphasis). This necessity depends
on the naive and unfounded assumptions that only the "stimula-
tive approaches" of manipulation and fellatio/cunnilingus are
available to the homosexual couple and that " . . . they are fundamentally my turn–your turn interactions as opposed to the 'our
turn' potential of coitus" (214). These mistaken premises ignore
the varieties of sexual techniques available to both homosexual
and heterosexual couples; the mutual and simultaneous possibilities in all techniques, including manipulation and oral sex; their
own finding that the giving of pleasure to a partner could be
sensual and exciting in the extreme; and, finally, the degree to
which heterosexual coitus, like any act between two people, can
be one-sided and selfish and not of an "our turn" nature.

Masters and Johnson's failure to recognize the heterosexual bias
that they deny so vigorously has grave implications for their
allegedly nonjudgmental and neutral therapeutic interactions. For
example, how "open" can a clinican/patient discussion of " . . .
the positive and/or negative contributions that the client's social

and sexual value systems are making to his or her life style" (334) be when the clinican thinks homosexuality has "long-term disadvantages?"

Masters and Johnson's belief that their therapy with the homosexually oriented is any less socially and subjectively weighted than that of preceding times is mistaken.

Results of Therapy.   Any discussion of the success or failure of the results reported by Masters and Johnson is problematic in the extreme. They stress that they are reporting only failure rates. This qualification is made even stronger by the insistence that a failure rate of 20 percent does not mean a success rate of 80 percent (381). Unfortunately, while they never explain just what the 80 percent does signify, they eventually treat it in their discussion as if it means success. To confuse matters even further, they never provide the criteria by which they judge this nondefined "nonfailure." In other words, discussion of therapy options is difficult because it is impossible to know exactly what Masters and Johnson are talking about. The paradoxical nature of their communication is further complicated by the misapplied and misleading statistics describing the seemingly detailed results.

Failure rates are reported for two groups, "reversion" and "conversion," and for two stages, after the completion of initial therapy and after long-term follow-up. Division into groups de-pends completely on an operational definition of heterosexual intercourse as synonymous with heterosexual orientation. Thus, the "reversion" group consists of those who had experienced heterosexual coitus at some previous time. Because of this experi-ence they are considered to have been heterosexual and to have become homosexual. The goal of therapy for this group, therefore, is a "reversion" to heterosexuality. On the other hand, the "conversion" candidates are those who had never experienced heterosexual coitus, thus were never heterosexual, and therefore are to be *converted* to heterosexuality.

The equation of a sexual act with a sexual orientation has already been discussed. A slightly different issue arises with the Masters and Johnson report, however. Although never specified, the implication is that exactly the same therapeutic and evaluative techniques were used with both groups. The immediate question is why the subjects were divided into two groups. Except for the insights provided into Masters and Johnson's concept of sexual orientation, the separation serves no apparent purpose. No important distinctions are drawn, nor are clinical or theoretical implications discussed. The only result is an increase in the numbers to be absorbed, compared, and juggled when trying to evaluate the supposed success that Masters and Johnson report even while they claim they are not reporting it.

With full recognition of the redundancy involved, it must be stressed that criteria for evaluation of failure or nonfailure are not given. Nor, as mentioned above, are failure or nonfailure ever defined. The implication, however, is that nonfailure, at least for the initial stage, is heterosexual performance to orgasm. For example, to describe one patient, "R ... did convert. He began functioning successfully in intercourse on the tenth day of therapy" (353).

Initial Failure Rates (IFR) are given for the first stage for males and females in "reversion" or "conversion" therapy. For males, IFR was 22 percent for conversion ($N = 9$) and 20 percent for reversion ($N = 45$); for females, IFR was 0 percent for conversion ($N = 3$) and 30 percent for reversion ($N = 10$) (393–396). Overall, IFR was 20.9 percent ($N = 67$). Again, there is no way to know what these figures mean, but the implication seems to be that 53 of the 67 subjects performed heterosexual intercourse at least once.

The Overall Failure Rate (OFR) after "long-term follow-up" is again reported for both males and females in "reversion" and "conversion" therapy: 26.7 percent of the males ($N = 45$) failed to revert to heterosexuality and 33.3 percent failed to convert ($N = 9$); 40 percent of the females ($N = 10$) failed to revert to heterosexuality while none failed to convert ($N = 3$). For males and females in both "reversion" and "conversion" therapy, the OFR was a reported 28.4 percent ($N = 67$).

Since Masters and Johnson insist that the 26.7 percent failure rate does *not* mean a 73.3 percent success rate, we again do not know what they are reporting and therefore cannot evaluate their claims. What is evident, however, are the conclusions they want the reader to draw. With their repeated use of terms like "treatment reversal" and return to a "prior homosexual orientation," the only inference possible is that, despite their disclaimers, nonfailure means attainment of a heterosexual as opposed to a homosexual orientation. To repeat, since criteria for IFR or OFR are never given, nor are terms like "treatment reversal" ever defined, we cannot evaluate the results and—just as importantly—we cannot attempt to replicate the treatment.

The nonmeaning of the text becomes almost inconsequential compared to the nonmeaning of the figures, however. Indeed, the statistical treatment of the data can only be called misdirection.

Repeatedly, Masters and Johnson stress the high motivation of their subjects. Yet, when discussing follow-up, they describe these highly motivated clients as follows:

> . . . a significant number of this group [those seeking sexual orientation change] had hardly been cooperative during the acute phase in therapy, and despite the fact that they had accomplished the preference alteration [sic] they had requested, they continued to be almost as uncooperative after therapy as they had been during treatment. (398)

Indeed, 19 of the 53 reported nonfailures in the initial stage were so uncooperative that they refused to take part in the follow-up. It is at this point that obfuscation becomes pseudoscientific jaberwocky. Masters and Johnson were faced with the problem of how to deal with these 19 supposed nonfailures. Instead of considering the obvious possibility that these 19 were "treatment reversals," or even excluding them from the final computations for OFR, they state that "a small number of these individuals could be expected to return to their prior homosexual orientation during the five-year period" (400). No explanation is given as to why only a "small number" might return to "their prior homosexual orientation." Nevertheless, operating on this unexplained assumption, they extrapolate from the five "treatment reversals" found in the patients who did cooperate in the nonspecified follow-up. They conclude that only four of the 19 no-shows were treatment reversals, presenting the remaining 15 as successes in their discussions of the data.

The indefensible inclusion of subjects who were never interviewed as nonfailures comes dangerously close to "fudging." The only defense that can be offered is that the inclusion was described and that there was no intent to mislead. Nevertheless, the misleading use of unjustifiable statistical extrapolation, the lack of specified criteria, and the ultimate incomprehensibility of the results lead to the inescapable conclusion that Masters and Johnson's claims for their "reversion" and "conversion" therapy are worthless.

IATROGENESIS AND OTHER CONSIDERATIONS

> ... the patient reluctantly visited a prostitute. Erection only after prolonged manipulation. Coitus performed with inner repugnance; intense physical reaction in an attack of migraine following the act. Great depression; suicidal thoughts. ... The patient continues to have violent migraines after hypnosis. (von Schrenk-Notzing 1896, 255)

> Even when such an attempt succeeds it is not usually possible to regard the results with much satisfaction. Not only is the acquisition of the normal instinct by an invert very much on the level of the acquisition of a vice, but probably it seldom succeeds in eradicating the original inverted instinct. What usually happens is that the person becomes capable of experiencing both impulses—not an especially satisfactory state of things. It may be disastrous especially if it leads to marriage, as it may do in an inverted man or still more easily in an inverted woman.[7] The apparent change does not turn out to be, and the invert's position is more unfortunate than his original position, both for himself and for his wife. (Havelock Ellis 1891, 333)

The weaknesses of these three approaches go far beyond flaws in reporting, research design, specificity of criteria, or reliability and validity. One crucial issue centers around the possible dangers these therapies represent for the patient they are ostensibly designed to help. The reports discussed above give no indication of the possible iatrogenic sequelae of attempts to change sexual orientation (Freund 1977).

Issues of iatrogensis and informed consent are not abstract

academic concerns but rather important professional and ethical issues that, at least in the area of change of sexual orientation, have long been neglected. Since therapy is not necessarily benign, professional and ethical standards demand at least informed consent on the part of the patient. To address these issues, we must return to the most fundamental clinical and theoretical question— what is being treated?

None of these three approaches deals with the role that internalized homophobia plays in the development of ego-dystonic homosexuality. Kaplan ignores it completely. Pattison and Pattison describe a therapy that actually tries to intensify the negative view of homosexuality and, thus, the phenomena associated with the diagnosis. Masters and Johnson touch on prejudice, but only as a source of motivation and as a rationalization for therapy. These theoretical and clinical lapses create the greatest iatrogenic danger. A clinician's implicit acceptance of the homosexual orientation as the cause of the ego-dystonic reactions, and the concomitant agreement to attempt sexual orientation change, exacerbates the ego-dystonic reactions and reinforces and confirms the internalized homophobia that lies at their root. Even more dangerous, they offer a false palliative that may have disastrous long-term effects.

The simplistic equation of sexual orientation with a sexual act, or the lack of a sexual act (Pattison and Pattison 1980), joins with neglect of the internalized homophobia to mask the meaning of the heterosexual act for the ego-dystonic homosexual. There is no lack of evidence that the homosexually oriented can successfully perform heterosexual coitus. For homosexuals who have identified with the dominant group, however, the desire to be like others is so strong that heterosexual coitus becomes more than an act of sex or love but a symbol of freedom (Martin 1982a; Goffman 1963). Successful heterosexual coitus may bring a release from tension that is so great that the possible sources of the relief are ignored. A feeling that one will no longer have to hide, that one can be a member of the Christian community to which one was raised, that one can become a parent, and perhaps most importantly that one need no longer be different are powerful incentives to believe that a sexual act signals the end of a homosexual orientation. When the ego-dystonic homosexual realizes that the vaunted decrease in homosexual behavior or heterosexual coitus does not mean a change in sexual orientation, depression, unhappiness, and even more devastating alienation may result.

Most of the patients discussed in these reports are men. It is impossible to know whether this represents the traditional lack of attention to lesbians in the literature or a lower frequency of ego-dystonic homosexuality among women with an attendant lower frequency of desire to change. Both are important questions in themselves. The former would demonstrate even further the social bias inherent in these therapies; the latter could have important implications for a sociological view of ego-dystonic homosexuality. The social implications of these therapies go beyond the homosexual, male or female, who desires to change. Perhaps the most tragic result of the false optimism resulting from a simplistic confusion between sexual behavior and sexual orientation is marriage by these supposedly cured homosexuals. None of these studies seems to attach any importance to effects on others, notably those who become spouses of these patients. Again, women are the main population to be ignored, since most attempts to change are directed toward men. This clinical shortsightedness may not have the conscious intention of belittling women, but it does exacerbate the common cultural belief that male sexuality, performance, and gratification are more important than female sexuality, performance, and gratification. In so doing, it denigrates women in general as well as creating the probability of unfortunate results for those who marry these supposedly cured homosexuals. Nor does this emphasis on priapic performance allow for any consideration of the children that may result (Gantz 1983).

The above objections relate only to those who have "succeeded" in these approaches. But even if we were to suspend judgment and accept such negligible results as the 3.6 percent success rate offered by Pattison and Pattison, what of the 96.4 percent who failed? What are the effects of failure on this group, especially when the patient has been told that change depends on his or her motivation, on religious faith (Pattison and Pattison 1980), or even more perniciously, on a personal choice (Masters and Johnson 1979, 357–359)?

The technique is similar to that used in certain religions. The believer is taught that all things are possible through faith. If the believer succeeds, then the teaching is self-evident and faith is justified; if the believer does not succeed, however, then he or she did not have enough faith. The phrasing is different in therapy, with the patient told that success depends on his or her "motivation" and "choice." In other words, in both therapy and religion, success or failure becomes the responsibility of the patient/believer. Unfortunately, clinicians pay little attention to the tactic's potential for negative outcomes in therapy, particularly for those already burdened with societally induced guilt and shame.

Leaving aside for the moment the very important observation that there is not an iota of evidence to support the simplistic notion that because one can perform heterosexually or homosexually under certain restricted conditions one can choose one's sexual orientation, what does it mean when the client, convinced that the choice is his or hers, either suffers a "treatment reversal" or never succeeds? Failure in any of these approaches—whether it is the failure to achieve "maturity" as a Christian, to "revert" or "convert," or to "cure" inhibition of sexual desire—must have ramifications for anyone suffering from the self-hatred demonstrated by the ego-dystonic homosexual. In addition to its pernicious effect on the patient, it also has the effect of inhibiting honest and open evaluation of the therapy itself because of its inordinate attention to the failure of the patient.

CONCLUSION

> "I agree with you," said the Duchess; "and the moral of that is—'Be what you would seem to be'—or, if you'd like it put more simply— 'Never imagine yourself not to be otherwise than what it might appear to others that what you were or might have been was not otherwise than what you had been would have appeared to them to be otherwise.'" (Lewis Carroll, *Alice in Wonderland*)

The only protection against scientific legitimization of prejudice is attention to the rigors of scientific method (Gould 1981; Mosse 1978; Barker-Benfield 1976; Haller and Haller 1974). The homosexually oriented have nothing to fear from science, but they have a great deal to fear from pseudoscience.

The dictionary defines *polemic* as an argument against a position; a controversy. The polemic has played a part in the evolution of scientific thought and practice since at least 150 B.C. when Hipparchus, the mathematician and astronomer who invented trigonometry, attacked Eratosthenes as imprecise. Indeed, Kuhn (1962) analyzes historical developments in science through the metaphor of warlike revolutions, with defenders and attackers battling over the primacy of a particular scientific model.

In recent years, the term polemic has gained a pejorative connotation in scientific discourse. The underlying assumption that empirical or clinical science must be above argument or dissent is both unfortunate and dangerous. This chapter may be considered as a polemic in that it challenges the theoretical, clinical, and ethical foundations of certain therapeutic attempts to change sexual orientation. The arguments are not new; neither are these so-called modern therapies. As long ago as the mid-nineteenth century, physicians used therapeutic techniques similar to those described by Masters and Johnson, Kaplan, and Pattison and Pattison to achieve exactly the same results, and their contemporaries were questioning the rationales and efficacy of those techniques. Every rationale or result implied in these approaches has been proposed, practiced, discussed, and dismissed before. Even the techniques for sexual dysfunction apparently utilized to enable the ego-dystonic homosexual to perform heterosexually were prefigured by nineteenth-century physicians dealing with problems of impotence (Haller and Haller 1974).

The difference between science and theology lies in the way the investigator uses the data with reference to his underlying belief system. The linking of homosexuality with the paraphilias because " . . . it makes more sense to me" (Kaplan 1983, 239); the unsupported assumption that homosexuality has "inherent long-range disadvantages" (Masters and Johnson 1979, 213); and the accusation that homosexuality is "psychological immaturity"

(Pattison and Pattison 1980) are all belief systems that, because of their social significance, need to be treated as hypotheses to be tested rather than as dogmatic givens that justify treatment. The APA has taken the stance that homosexuality is not a mental disorder. Clinicians who continue to treat it as a disorder have the professional and ethical obligation to justify their rationale and their treatment in the most rigorous fashion possible.

Science does not demand that an investigator or clinician be right, merely that they follow the rules. The implicit understanding is that if those rules are followed, a mistaken theoretical stance will be refuted eventually. Review of the literature, specification of criteria, attention to reliability and validity, logical consistency, appropriate analytic tools, and adequate reporting are not too much to ask of clinician researchers who propose treatment approaches with such important implications for patients, for those who will interact with those patients, and for society at large.

References

Allport G: The Nature of Prejudice. Garden City, NY, Doubleday, 1958

American Psychiatric Association: Diagnostic and Statistical Manual of Mental Disorders, 3rd ed. Washington, DC: American Psychiatric Association, 1980

Barker-Benfield GJ: The Horrors of the Half Known Life: Male Attitudes Toward Women and Sexuality in Nineteenth Century America. New York, Harper and Row, 1976

Bayer R: Homosexuality and American Psychiatry: The Politics of Diagnosis. New York, Basic Books, 1981

Bell AP, Weinberg MS: Homosexualities: A Study of Diversity Among Men and Women. New York, Simon and Schuster, 1978

Berg C, Allen C: The Problem of Homosexuality. New York, Citadel Press, 1958

Bieber I, Dain H, Dince P, et al: Homosexuality: A Psychoanalytic Study of Male Homosexuals. New York, Basic Books, 1962

Blair R: Ex-Gay. New York, Homosexual Community Counseling Center, 1982

Bloch I: The Sexual Life of Our Time. Translated by Paul ME. New York, Rebman Co., 1908

Boone P: Coming Out: True Stories of the Gay Exodus. Van Nuys, Calif, Bible Voice, 1978

Curran D, Parr D: Homosexuality: An Analysis of 100 Male Cases Seen in Private Practice. Br Med J 5022:797–801, 1957

Duberman M: Homosexuality in Perspective by William H. Masters and Virginia E. Johnson [book review]. The New Republic 180:24–31, 1979

Ellis H (1891): Sexual inversion. [Republished in Studies in the Psychology of Sex. New York, Random House, 1936]

Feldman MP, MacCullough MJ: Homosexual Behavior: Therapy and Assessment. New York, Pergamon Press, 1971

Ferenczi S: The nosology of male homosexuality, in Sex in Psychoanalysis: Contributions to Psychoanalysis. Translated by Jones E. Boston, Gorham Press, 1916, pp 296–318

Forel A: The Sexual Question: A Scientific, Psychological, Hygienic and Sociological Study. Translated by Marshall CF. New York, Rebman Co, 1911 [German text, 1905]

Freud S (1905): Three essays on a theory of sexuality, in The Standard Edition of the Complete Psychological Works of Sigmund Freud, Volume 7. Translated and edited by James Strachey. London, Hogarth Press, 1953

Freund K: Should homosexuality arouse therapeutic concern? J Homosex 2(3):235–240, 1977

Gangel K: The Gospel and the Gay. New York, Thomas Nelson, 1978

Gantz J: Whose Child Cries? Rolling Hills Estates, Calif, Jalmar Press, 1983

Goffman E: Stigma: Notes on the Management of Spoiled Identity. Engelwood Cliffs, NJ, Prentice Hall, 1963

Gould, SJ: The Mismeasure of Man. New York, Norton and Norton, 1981

Greenberg JS: A study of male homosexuals. Journal of the American College Health Association 22:56–60, 1973

Haller J, Haller R: The Physician and Sexuality in Victorian America. Urbana, University of Illinois Press, 1974

Hellman RE, Green R, Gray JL, et al: Childhood sexual identity, childhood religiosity and 'homophobia' as influences in the development of transexualism, homosexuality, and heterosexuality. Arch Gen Psychiatry 38:910–915, 1981

Hetrick ES, Martin AD: More on "ex-gays." Am J Psychiatry 138:1510–1511, 1981

Kaplan HS: The New Sex Therapy. New York, Brunner/Mazel, 1974

Kaplan HS: Disorders of Sexual Desire. New York, Simon and Schuster, 1979

Kaplan HS: ISD: a model for the treatment of egodystonic homosexuality. Unpublished paper presented at the 2nd symposium in the Integrative Psychiatry Series, held at New York Medical College, January 1982

Kaplan HS: The Evaluation of Sexual Disorders. New York, Brunner/Mazel, 1983

Kardiner A: Sex and Morality. New York, Bobbs Merrill, 1954

von Krafft-Ebing R (1896): Psychopathia Sexualis. Translated by Klaf FS from the 12th German edition. New York, Bell Publishing Co, 1965

Kronemeyer R: Overcoming Homosexuality. New York, Macmillian, 1980

Kuhn T: The Structure of Scientific Revolution. Chicago, University of Chicago Press, 1962

LaHaye T: What Everyone Should Know About Homosexuality. Wheaton, Ill, Tyndale House Publishers, 1980

Larsen KS, Cate R, Reed M: Anti-black attitudes, religious orthodoxy, permissiveness, and sexual information: a study of the attitudes of heterosexuals toward homosexuality. Journal of Sex Research 19:105–118, 1983

Martin AD: The minority question. etcetera 39:22–42, 1982a

Martin AD: Learning to hide: the socialization of the gay adolescent, in Adolescent Psychiatry: Developmental and Clinical Studies, Vol 10. Edited by Feinstein SC, Looney JG, Schwartzberg AZ, et al. Chicago, University of Chicago Press, 1982b

Masters WH, Johnson VE: Homosexuality in Perspective. Boston, Little, Brown, 1979

Moll A: Libido Sexualis. [German edition, 1897, Untersuchungen über die Libido Sexualis.] Translated by Berger D. New York, American Ethnological Press, 1933

Moore TV: The pathogenesis and treatment of homosexual disorders: a digest of some pertinent evidence. J Pers 14:47–83, 1945

Morris P: Shadow of Sodom: Facing the Facts of Homosexuality. Wheaton, Ill, Tyndale House Publishers, 1978

Mosse GL: Toward the Final Solution: A History of European Racism. New York, Howard Fertig, 1978

Offer, D, Sabshin M, Offer J: Normality: Theoretical Concepts of Mental Health. New York, Basic Books, 1974

Owensby, NM: Homosexuality and lesbianism treated with metrazol. J Nerv Ment Dis 92:65–66, 1940

Owensby NM: The correction of homosexuality. Urologic and Cutaneous Review 45:494–496, 1941

Parr D: Homosexuality in clinical practice. Proc R Soc Med 50:651–654, 1957

Pattison EM: Confusing concepts about the concept of homosexuality. Psychiatry 37:340–349, 1974

Pattison EM: Positive though inaccurate. Journal of American Scientific Affiliation 29:106–108, 1977

Pattison EM, Pattison ML: "Ex-gays": religiously mediated change in homosexuals. Am J Psychiatry 137:1553–1562, 1980

Philpott K: The Third Sex. Plainfield, NJ, Logos International, 1975

Philpott K: The Gay Theology. Plainfield, NJ, Logos International, 1977

Saghir MT, Robins E: Male and Female Homosexuality. Baltimore, Williams and Wilkins, 1973

von Schrenck-Notzing A: Die Suggestions-therapie bei krankhaften Erscheinungen des Geschlechtssinnes: mit besonderer Berücksichtigung der contraren Sexualempfindung. Stuttgart, Ferdinand Enke, 1892 [English version: Therapeutic Suggestion in Psychopathia Sexualis with Especial Reference to Contrary Sexual Instinct. Philadelphia, FA Davis, 1895]

Schwartz MF, Masters WH: The Masters and Johnson treatment program for dissatisfied homosexual men. Am J Psychiatry 141:173–181, 1984

Socarides CW: Homosexuality. New York, Jason Aronson, 1978

Socarides CW: Psychoanalytic perspectives on female homosexuality: a discussion of "the lesbian as a 'single' woman." Am J Psychotherapy 35:510–515, 1981

Stekel W: Onanie and Homosexualität. [Part 1: Bisexual love. Part 2: The homosexual neurosis.] Translated by Van Teslaar J. Boston, Gorham Press, 1922

Sulloway FJ: Freud: biologist of the mind. New York, Basic Books, 1979

Symonds JA (1896): A Problem in Modern Ethics. Reprinted in Homosexuality, A Cross Cultural Approach. Edited by Cory DW. New York, Julian Press, 1955

Thompson GN: Electroshock and other therapeutic considerations in sexual psychopathy. J Nerv Ment Dis 109:531–539, 1949

Tripp CA: The Homosexual Matrix. New York, McGraw Hill, 1975

Ulrichs K: Memnon. Die Geschlechtsnatur des mannliebenden Urnings: Eine naturwissenschaftliche Darstellung 1868. Cited in Symonds 1896 (above).

Vanderveldt, JH, Odenwald RP: Psychiatry and Catholicism. 2nd ed. New York, McGraw Hill, 1975

Weinberg, M, Williams C: Male homosexuals. New York, Oxford University Press, 1974

Wilson WP: Biology, psychology and homosexuality, in What You Should Know About Homosexuality. Edited by Keysor CW. Grand Rapids, Zondervan, 1979

Zilbergeld B, Evans M: The inadequacy of Masters and Johnson. Psychology Today 14:29–43, 1980

Notes

[1]This consistent finding is interpreted in a different way by those like Socarides (1978, 1981) and Vanderveldt and Odenwald (1957), who believe that since homosexuality is an illness that must bring unhappiness, any homosexual who says he or she is happy is obviously very sick and even more desperately in need of help.

[2]Some of the material in this section was previously published in a letter to the editor of the *American Journal of Psychiatry* (Hetrick and Martin 1981).

[3]The impact of social Darwinism on theories of sexual development, and especially on theories of the development of homosexuality, is most clearly seen in psychodynamic formulations. In 1958, a psychoanalyst who considered himself an expert in changing homosexuals to heterosexuals wrote:

> We have the behavior of the monkeys and apes, who pass through a stage before maturity in which they show homosexual activity. One might expect something similar in human beings. Such a similarity is found in the behavior of savages, many of whom have homosexual customs. . . . By analogy with monkeys and apes, homosexuality is immaturity, and the adult ape drops it because he finds copulation with the female more enjoyable. *Since man has evolved from the apes, it is not surprising if we find that he retains some residue of his development* [emphasis his]. If homosexuality occurs in monkeys and apes, as we have shown, then we should expect that it might be prevalent in primitive races [sic] and in very early historical times. (Berg and Allen 1958, 20)

See Sulloway (1979) for a complete discussion of the influence of nineteenth-century biological formulations on Freud's psychological theories.

[4]It must be stressed that, considering the number of sects in Christianity, a term like "Christian Community" can have only idiosyncratic meaning. It should also be noted that while Judaism

seems to have no equivalent to the Christian "ex-gay" movement, antigay pressures within the Jewish community often center around similar issues of group membership.

[5]While Bieber and his colleagues claim a complete change to a heterosexual orientation for 19 percent of exclusively homosexual and 50 percent of the bisexual patients, they offer no evidence other than assertion. Nor do they list criteria for evaluating the reported change (change reported by the analyst, not the patient); nor do they indicate how follow-up, if any, was carried out. Years later Bieber admitted that of all the claimed cures only one might fulfill the Kinsey criteria for documented change. This one patient could not be examined, however, because he was not on speaking terms with his analyst (Tripp 1975, 251). Some of the inadequacies of Feldman and MacCullough have already been noted.

[6]Many of the points discussed in this section were first raised by Martin Duberman (1979) in his *New Republic* review of *Homosexuality in Perspective*. An essay in *Psychology Today* (Zilbergeld and Evans 1980) pointed out difficulties in the reporting of the data and thus the replicability of Masters and Johnson's work on sexual dysfunction with heterosexuals. Both essays stressed a point not addressed here, whether the "dissatisfied homosexuals" were bisexual. While diagnostic classifications are important, I feel the question of bisexuality merely takes away from the main point, the complete lack of scientific adequacy in these reports.

[7]Ellis was, unhappily, speaking from experience. He had married a lesbian, and although they reached an understanding, her affairs with women caused him great distress.

3

Psychotherapy with Gay Men and Lesbians: An Examination of Homophobia, Coming Out, and Identity

Terry S. Stein, M.D.
Carol J. Cohen, M.D.

3

Psychotherapy with Gay Men and Lesbians: An Examination of Homophobia, Coming Out, and Identity

In the more than ten years since the American Psychiatric Association eliminated homosexuality as a diagnosis of mental illness, the psychiatric literature has been relatively silent regarding psychotherapy with gay men and lesbians. This chapter represents an effort to begin to explore some of the specific issues that arise for this population during psychotherapy, with a special focus on the pivotal roles of coming out and homophobia.

The authors believe that scientific study has adequately refuted the idea that homosexuality per se is in any way inherently pathological (Bell and Weinberg 1978; Mitchell 1978). The refusal by a psychotherapist to accept the fact that homosexuality is a normal variation of human behavior must at this point be viewed as an absolute barrier to working with gay men and lesbians in psychotherapy. This refusal is rooted in a deeply held internalized homophobia. *Homophobia* is a term that was originally used by Weinberg (1972) and refers to the fear or rejection of homosexuality and of persons who are homosexual. Homophobic attitudes can occur within psychotherapy both in the transference and in the countertransference. If the homophobic reactions are not made conscious and worked through, the results will be especially devastating to the gay man or lesbian who is coming out.

Coming out is a developmental process that leads to a person's identification as a gay man or lesbian. The relevance of coming out to achieving a healthy gay identity has only recently been recognized. Just as feminine psychology cannot be understood solely by comparison with or distillation from masculine psychology, identity development for homosexuals cannot be understood simply by comparison with heterosexuals. Homosexuality is associated with certain societal experiences and individual developmental tasks which together shape and comprise the coming out process. These experiences and tasks are distinctly different from those associated with heterosexual development in our society. This fact has great relevance for conducting psychotherapy with gay male and lesbian patients.

Coming out involves stepping out of the metaphorical closet where one has hidden one's homosexuality from others and from oneself. This process is not possible for a primarily heterosexual person simply because there is no similar need to hide heterosexuality in this society. Thus, in coming out, the gay man or lesbian must reclaim disowned or devalued parts of the self. The effects of societal pressure to be heterosexual have often been to inculcate a basic mistrust or hatred for one's sexual and interpersonal identity when it is homosexual. A therapist who further encourages renunciation or denial of the homosexual feelings may destructively reinforce the patient's own internalized homophobia. There are no truly parallel risks of the therapist's judgment for the heterosexual person who is in treatment.

Sexual orientation itself does not represent a simply dichotomous categorization of persons into homosexual and heterosexual or gay and straight groups. Kinsey demonstrated that individual sexual behavior and attraction can be described on a continuum between exclusively homosexual and exclusively heterosexual (Kinsey et al. 1948; Kinsey et al. 1953). DeCecco (1981) has discussed how the individual's experience of sexual orientation actually involves more than one continuum, including at least sexual behavior, erotic fantasies, and interpersonal affection, as well as historical changes in a person's location on these continua over the course of a lifetime. Studies have shown that coming out as a gay man or lesbian also comprises a complicated series of events that both affect and are shaped by many other aspects of a person's life. Coming out is indeed a "life process" (Woodman and Lenna 1980), which is related not only to sexual behavior but also to experiences of fantasy and relational preference in addition to many other aspects of self-identity.

McDonald (1982) has discussed how a conceptualization of coming out as a linear progressive continuum is not adequate because of the obstacles presented by both internal and external prohibitions against coming out. Persons cannot usually simply progress in a sequential manner through a series of stages of awareness about one's sexual orientation which eventually leads to a full acknowledgment and acceptance of a homosexual orientation. It is the nonlinear progress in a sequential manner through a series of stages of awareness about one's sexual orientation that eventually leads to a full acknowledgment and acceptance of a homosexual orientation. The nonlinear progression is due in part to individual variations and in part to social, political, and interpersonal forces that work against such development. Any examination of the coming out process as it might occur during the course of individual psychotherapy must therefore also pay attention to these countervailing forces. These forces will be experienced outside therapy in the family, the work setting, and the larger society, and they will be brought into therapy by both patient and therapist in the form of internalized homophobia.

The internalization of homophobia significantly influences identity development in gay men and lesbians whether they are in psychotherapy or not. Most gay men and lesbians will incorporate society's antigay attitudes into their sense of self-identity. As with the term *racism*, the origins and development of the attitudes referred to as homophobic are not explained by the term itself. The homophobic reactions of individuals and social agencies can be labeled as internalized and institutional homophobia respectively (Hencken 1982).

The origins of homophobia are deep-rooted and related to the development of gender roles and gender identity in our society. In this culture male and female are defined as opposites in important parameters, and one finds identity in the one group frequently by eschewing any similarity to the other group. Since the social stereotype of the homosexual involves the presence of traits of the opposite sex (for example, the "effeminate" gay man and the "butch" lesbian [Ettorre 1980]), adamant rejection of homosexuality is consistent with the development of gender identity and gender role (Morin and Garfinkle 1978). This rejection is maintained as a form of internalized homophobia by all members of the society, both gay and nongay. Rejection of the stereotypes of gay men and lesbians in association with an individual sense of identity as being male or female persists despite the fact that very few homosexuals have been shown to resemble these reductive characterizations.

At a cultural level, homophobia leads to the attribution of rejected, denigrated, or feared characteristics to homosexuals as a group. This represents an effort to render homosexuals entirely unlike heterosexuals. Differences are thereby institutionalized as society rejects unwanted characteristics and views them as belonging to a minority group (de Monteflores 1982). Examples of characteristics that are impugned to the group of homosexual persons include promiscuity, inability to maintain intimate adult relationships, seductiveness towards children, and extreme narcissism. Any gay man or lesbian who actually conforms to the expected negative image is seen as confirming the derogatory stereotypes of homosexuals as a group. Ignoring the role of stereotyping allows heterosexuality to be viewed as the required road to health and intimacy. Again, obvious parallels exist between this situation and the development of racist attitudes and their function in maintaining a sense of identity of one group, the majority, at the expense of another group, the minority.

In psychiatry, Marmor (1980) has pointed out how traditional beliefs about the pathology of gay people have served to provide a so-called scientific validation for discrimination against these persons and to perpetuate a homophobic mythology. Malyon (1982) has discussed some of the implications for psychotherapy of internalized homophobia with gay men. As long as reactions against homosexuality persist as pervasive elements in individual identity and as widespread social attitudes, they will inevitably continue to occur during psychotherapy with gay men and lesbians as well.

Yet despite the centrality of homophobia in our culture, only recently have its myriad effects on individuals been studied. The existence of some specific homophobic reactions in psychotherapy has been suggested by Davison and Friedman (1981). Their study demonstrated a distortion in judgment about hypothetical cases which results from stereotyping on the basis of sexual orientation. In their study men who were described as having engaged in homosexual relationships were diagnosed more frequently as having nonsexual psychological problems caused by their unconventional homosexual life-style. Identical case histories were judged as healthier if the patients were labeled as heterosexual. These results demonstrate one type of clinical distortion that can result from homophobia.

The individual and cultural homophobic attitudes cannot be expected to disappear magically upon entrance into the therapist's office, either for the therapist or the patient. However, even though studies have shown that clinical judgment can be significantly altered as a function of the therapist knowing the patient's sexual orientation, such awareness of sexual orientation cannot actually predict other crucial aspects of the person that should be the fabric of an evaluation of relative health or illness. These other parameters include level of ego development, type of character, and style of relating to others.

Several clinical examples and situations will serve to illustrate how homophobia occurs in therapy with patients who are coming out. Both homophobia and coming out can be seen as complex processes that are experienced by all gay men and lesbians in some form. They weave through the unique dynamics, conflicts, developmental history, and transference of the individual in therapy. Certain reactions and experiences of therapists also illustrate how therapy can be hindered or facilitated by the therapist's awareness of homophobic countertransference reactions. All of the clinical situations in the following section are taken from the authors' experience.

CLINICAL DISCUSSION

Perhaps the most obvious manifestation of homophobia within psychotherapy occurs as part of the therapist's countertransference reactions to the patient's initial explorations of homosexual feelings. As a result of this reaction, a therapist may respond to concerns about homosexual feelings with reductionistic statements that serve to block the patient's efforts to talk about the subject. An example of this phenomenon would be when a therapist tells a patient to discount any homosexual feelings because he or she is orgasmic during heterosexual intercourse. Such statements might serve to bind the therapist's anxiety about homosexuality by neatly separating homosexual and heterosexual feelings into mutually exclusive realms and thereby avoiding the complexity and ambiguity that actually exists about the topic of sexual orientation; however, they would only frustrate the patient.

A less obvious but equally important manifestation of homophobia in psychotherapy occurs when the therapist avoids discussion of the patient's negative feelings about homosexuality and only permits exploration of positive feelings about the subject. Although such a strategy may be chosen in order to protect the patient from painful effects, ultimately it serves only to truncate the patient's experience.

Negative feelings may occur at certain points in the coming out process when a significant change in a person's identity takes place. Such a change, by upsetting the equilibrium of the person's previous sense of self, can often involve a period of significant ambivalence, self-doubt, and temporary lowering of self-esteem. This period may be brief or protracted, and for the person in therapy its course can be strongly affected by how the therapist responds to concerns that arise for the patient. Ambivalence about coming out has one root in the internalization of the societal judgments that homosexuality is sick, morally wrong, or at best inferior to heterosexuality—in short, the patient's internalized homophobia. The therapist must encourage exploration of these negative feelings, which may occur during the coming out process, both by acknowledging the reality of external prohibitions against homosexuality and by understanding that the internal judgments have frequently become more potent and meaningful restrictions for the patient.

Another common error of the therapist in this situation is to assume that the patient's ambivalence about coming out indicates that he or she is not really a gay man or lesbian. However, since such periods of ambivalence are painful but frequently necessary way stations in any process of change, it is crucial that the therapist not mistakenly view the ambivalence as a cue to reaffirm the patient's heterosexuality.

Some patients who are coming out and experiencing changes in personal identity may experiment in various aspects of their lives. For example, marked changes in style of dress or withdrawal from a previously established social network may be observed. Such shifts are best regarded by the therapist as useful external indicators of internal change. Ultimately such experimentation can provide a basis for making significant decisions aimed at finding greater permanent support for a new life-style. Some patients may realistically consider changing jobs or moving to geographic locations where other gay persons are more easily found. The therapist working with gay men and lesbians must be aware that some locations, such as small towns, rural areas and even certain cities, may be relatively oppressive for the person who is seeking to develop a positive identity as a gay person.

In summary, these examples illustrate the first important clinical point for therapists who work with gay men and lesbians: the therapist must be careful not to block either the positive or negative reactions that patients have as they explore their homosexual feelings. Both sides of the ambivalence that occurs during the coming out process must be allowed expression if the patient is to develop an integrated sense of self as a gay man or lesbian. Discussing this ambivalence and tolerating the confusion about life-style choices may be extremely difficult because of internalized homophobia in both the patient and the therapist.

A second important clinical point for therapists working with gay men and lesbian patients is that many of them may project their ambivalence and fears about coming out—expressions of internalized homophobia—onto social settings or significant others in order to defend against some other psychological problem or conflict that does not directly relate to their sexual orientation. The following example demonstrates such a situation.

[Case 1]: A successful professional man was secretive and ashamed about his homosexuality. He ascribed these feelings to his concern that he not jeopardize the aspiration of his brother to be a career military officer. As a result, he limited his own relationships to brief affairs. The therapist encouraged exploration of the patient's feelings about the situation rather than simply accepting the perceptions about a need to protect his brother. Ultimately the underlying difficulty was seen to be the patient's rigid obsessive defenses, which were aimed at a strict regulation of any expression of intimacy or dependency.

The patient viewed close relationships as potentially dangerous and disruptive to his sense of self. This view had its origins in the trauma he experienced at the time of his parents' bitter divorce when he was five years old. The issue of homosexuality was realistically difficult within the patient's family context, but the issues of control and ego boundaries raised in any type of relationship were more important for this individual. The therapist's recognition that the patient's internalized homophobia was an expression of another intrapsychic conflict while at the same time acknowledging the realistic fears of a familial stigma facilitated a resolution of the patient's problems. Eventually this man was able to establish lasting close relationships with other men as well as to achieve an improved self-esteem and greater effectiveness in his profession.

This case illustrates how a patient can use internalized homophobia as a defense against other conflicts, such as a prohibition against a wished-for intimacy. Affirming the realistic nature of a concern about possible societal reactions is often an important preliminary step which can lead to further exploration of the internalized homophobia and associated guilt about homosexuality. The experience of deviancy in a predominantly heterosexual society cannot therefore be ignored, but neither should such experiences be used to avoid exploration of other internal processes including the deep, self-defeating reactions to such social stigma. For many patients, other intrapsychic and developmental conflicts will eventually be seen to be the primary source of current symptoms and difficulties. Internalized homophobia is thus an important personality feature to be explored within psychotherapy, but it may also serve as a defense against other conflicts that do not directly relate to the patient's sexual orientation.

A third clinical point is that gay male and lesbian patients may, for complex reasons, frequently view the therapist as the repository of societal and familial prohibitions against homosexuality and as a result may develop a generalized negative transference to the therapist. At its most extreme, such a reaction when unacknowledged may lead to premature termination of therapy and to avoidance of the subject of homosexuality altogether within therapy. In such a situation, the patient may believe that she or he is protecting against the therapist's inability to understand deeply held feelings. Of course, this defensive maneuver leads only to an incomplete therapy in which two key issues—coming out and the negative transference—are both unable to be worked through. To prevent these outcomes the therapist must think about what the patient is *not* saying, especially when details about important object relationships appear to be missing. Moreover, the therapist must never make the error of assuming that a patient is primarily or exclusively heterosexual. Sometimes patients may consciously believe that they are protecting the therapist from confronting the subject of homosexuality. The following example describes a patient who reenacted a major psychodynamic theme from her past through this maneuver.

[Case 2]: A 24-year-old woman graduate student entered therapy with a male psychiatrist, complaining of difficulties in getting along with her male colleagues. The therapist focused on the competitive aspects of her situation, drawing on the patient's background which included a difficult relationship to a somewhat sadistic older brother. This material was not translated into possible transferential implications, such as the patient's fantasies about the therapist's own need to be

powerful and his possible underlying insecurities. The patient viewed this therapist as helpful in narrowly defined areas, such as her conflicts with fellow students, but very conservative in his attitudes. She believed that he would disapprove of homosexuality. Weekly therapy continued for two years until the patient moved to another location to pursue her career. The fact that she had been coming out as a lesbian during this course of therapy was never mentioned except to a few close friends.

Several years later, in therapy again and at another point in her coming out process, the patient was able to acknowledge that she had been afraid of damaging the first therapist, of differentiating from him, in this case by acknowledging her lesbian identity and thereby presumably being shown to be different from him. The genetic roots for her avoidance and negative projections were subsequently traced back to her playing a maternal role to a seriously depressed mother. The patient had unconsciously seen all objects as fragile and needing to be protected from an awareness of her sexual individuation.

The patient's second therapist pursued the transference reactions more actively and thereby helped uncover the central dynamic conflicts for this woman. The first therapist had essentially colluded with the patient to avoid material about homosexuality, differentiation, and fear of aggression. The patient's omission of material about coming out during the first therapy was a conscious process; however, the motivation for her secrecy derived from unconscious conflicts. To summarize, then, in order to work with lesbian and gay male patients, the therapist may frequently have to be attuned to what is not being said and may have to ask about negative feelings toward the therapist as well as about details that appear to be missing regarding important object relationships.

A fourth clinical point is that sexual behavior itself may present problems for the gay male or lesbian patient. Considering the intensity and pervasiveness of cultural pressures to demonstrate an active sexuality, it is not surprising that many patients, regardless of their sexual orientation, frequently present with difficulties integrating sexuality and emotional intimacy. The person who is initially coming out as a gay man or lesbian may be particularly sensitive to the quality of sexual experiences and concerned about the connection between sexuality and intimacy. It is important that the therapist who works with these patients be familiar with the varieties of sexual behavior that may occur and express a willingness to explore such matters.

Discussions of sexuality with a gay man or lesbian should provide a balanced point of view so that sexual behavior is neither overvalued nor undervalued as part of the emerging identity. At times, explicit discussion of sexual practices and fantasies may be useful, but an exclusive attention to sexuality may reinforce stereotypes of gay men and lesbians as being hypersexual or obsessed with sexuality. Because information about gay male and lesbian sexual practices tends to be limited and negatively biased, the therapist should be informed about resources such as publications and support groups. These resources can help patients become more realistically informed about their sexuality. The therapist's awareness about and nonjudgmental reactions to sexual practices among gay persons can provide a powerful bridge into an area bound to be filled with misinformation and colored by stigma. The therapist who can first allow the expression of concerns about negative attitudes, fears, and misinformation can then more easily suggest other points of view. In this way, internalized stereotypes about sexual behaviors can be more easily explored and worked through.

A final example will illustrate some of the complex connections that can exist between sexual orientation, coming out, homophobia, and all other aspects of a person's life.

[Case 3]: A married professional man entered therapy following his arrest for homosexual entrapment. In the course of evaluation the patient stated that he had no awareness of conflict regarding being homosexual. However, he clearly segmented his life into two parts, one involving a secret network of homosexual friends and frequently anonymous sexual encounters and the other his marriage and professional life. In the two years prior to his arrest, his children had left home, he had changed jobs, and he had moved. All of these changes and an associated pressure for greater intimacy with his wife had led to a frequent compulsive seeking after anonymous sex with men.

In the course of therapy, exploration of this man's previously unacknowledged internalized homophobia, which was obscured by a conscious acceptance of his homosexual feelings and behavior, demonstrated how he had in fact throughout his life used his compulsive and guilt-ridden homosexual behavior as a repository for painful and negative feelings, such as anxiety and feelings associated with low self-esteem. Through such conscious acceptance of homosexuality and unconscious internalization of homophobic attitudes, this man truncated possible experiences of intimacy both in his marriage to a woman and as a gay man. The exploration of these feelings led to his telling his wife about his being homosexual, to a total cessation of his compulsive sexual behavior, and ultimately to a greater capacity for intimacy with other persons. All aspects of his intrapsychic and developmental conflicts were eventually shown to be related to how he managed his homosexuality.

This example shows how internalized homophobia can be incorporated at an unconscious level and then can serve to keep the patient unaware of large parts of his or her experience. The homosexual experiences, when they are kept rigidly segmented off from the rest of the person's life, can become the repository for a whole set of negatively associated feelings and behaviors. As long as they remain consciously approved but unconsciously devalued, an integrated experience of intimacy within any relationship may be impossible because of a profound self-hatred. Resolution of this conflict can only occur through an acknowledgment of the deeply ingrained internalized homophobia and an incorporation of the sealed off aspects of identity into one's sense of self. Decisions about relationships and other aspects of a person's life-style can then be made based upon an awareness of realistic choices and consequences and not as a result of a pervasive unconscious self-hatred.

DISCUSSION

Far more questions have been raised in this chapter than have been answered. The authors have been concerned primarily, especially in the clinical discussion, with presenting new ways of looking at the issues and problems that gay men and lesbians bring to psychotherapy. There has been no attempt to categorize these concerns, and detailed examination of diagnosis, psychodynamic formulations, and overall approaches to treatment with gay male and lesbian patients has been left for later exploration. The central point of this chapter is that an intricate web of antihomosexual reactions has been woven into the identity of virtually every person in this society through the internalization of a profound cultural homophobia. Psychotherapists and patients alike must work to recognize these attitudes.

To reiterate the suggestions for sound clinical practices with lesbian and gay male patients that have been made in this chapter, four major clinical assertions have been presented:

1. Both positive and negative feelings about a homosexual identity will exist and should be explored within psychotherapy.
2. A patient's internalized homophobia often functions as a defense against other psychological conflicts and interpersonal problems.
3. A patient may view the therapist as the repository of societal and familial prohibitions against homosexuality and as a result may develop a strongly negative transference which is difficult to resolve.
4. The area of actual sexual behaviors may be particularly difficult for the gay male or lesbian patient to discuss. The therapist should be comfortable enough to encourage discussion in this area and should provide information when needed.

An understanding of the relevance of these points for conducting psychotherapy with gay male and lesbian patients should help the therapist to approach these men and women with respect and understanding as well as with greater effectiveness.

References

Bell A, Weinberg M: A Study of Diversity Among Men and Women. New York, Simon and Schuster, 1978

Davison G, Friedman S: Sexual orientation stereotype in the distortion of clinical judgment. J Homosex 6:37–44, 1981

DeCecco J: Definition and meaning of sexual orientation. J Homosex 6:51–67, 1981

de Monteflores C: Notes on the management of difference. Presented at the American Orthopsychiatric Association Annual Meeting, San Francisco, 1982

Ettorre E: Lesbians, Women and Society. London, Routledge & Kegan Paul, 1980

Hencken J: Homosexuality and psychoanalysis: toward a mutual understanding, in Homosexuality: Social, Psychological and Biological Issues. Edited by Weinrich PW Jr, et al. Beverly Hills, Sage Publications, 1982

Kinsey AC, Pomeroy WB, Martin CE: Sexual Behavior in the Human Male. Philadelphia, WB Saunders Co, 1948

Kinsey AC, Pomeroy WB, Martin CW, et al.: Sexual Behavior in the Human Female. Philadelphia, WB Saunders Co, 1953

Malyon A: Psychotherapeutic implications of internalized homophobia in gay men. J Homosex 7:59–70, 1982

Marmor J: Homosexual Behavior. New York, Basic Books, 1980

McDonald G: Individual differences in the coming out process for gay men: implications for theoretical models. J Homosex 8:47–60, 1982

Mitchell S: Psychodynamics, homosexuality, and the question of pathology. Psychiatry 41:251–263, 1978

Morin S, Garfinkle E: Male homophobia. Journal of Social Issues, 34:29–46, 1978

Weinberg G: Society and the Healthy Homosexual. New York, Anchor, 1972

Woodman N, Lenna H: Counseling with Gay Men and Women. San Francisco, Jossey-Bass, 1980

4

Psychotherapy With Gay And Lesbian Patients

James P. Krajeski, M.D.

4

Psychotherapy With Gay And Lesbian Patients

INTRODUCTION

Several factors have resulted in a need to review and update our knowledge of psychotherapy with gay men and lesbians. Significant among these factors was the removal of homosexuality as a mental disorder from DSM-III in 1973. Considerable controversy surrounded this change, and to some degree this controversy continues in spite of research findings strongly supporting a nonpathological view of homosexuality (Adelman 1977; Bell and Weinberg 1978; Clark 1975; Hart 1978; Meredith and Reister 1980).

The Gay Liberation movement, which has criticized psychiatry's view and treatment of homosexual men and women, has been a vocal force against the pathological concepts of homosexuality which some psychiatrists continue to advocate. Psychiatrists have been criticized for failing to speak with gay people rather than about them and for failing to look at nonclinical populations rather than drawing conclusions about gay people from clinical samples. Psychiatrists have been accused of homophobia, bias, prejudice, a lack of sensitivity, and a lack of knowledge of gay issues.

Still another force following in the path of the Gay Liberation movement has been the increased visibility of gay psychiatrists within the psychiatric profession. The openness and the participation of this group within organized psychiatry make it difficult to speak any longer of "them." Psychiatrists must instead speak about "you" or even "us" when referring to gay people. Psychiatrists are now told by their peers that they often do not understand gay people and that there is an urgent need to reexamine and update the traditional psychiatric approach to the gay patient.

Some of the criticisms of psychiatry may be valid, and some may not be. In any event, it is important that the psychiatrist's approach to the gay or lesbian patient is respectful, informed, and constructive. The recommendations and guidelines for psychotherapy with the gay or lesbian patient contained in this article are based on a broad perspective gained through a largely gay psychiatric practice, extensive contacts within the gay community, considerable discussion with both gay and nongay mental health professionals, and a review of the research literature.

It is essential to keep in mind that speaking about both gay men and lesbians as a single group may give a false impression of greater similarity between these groups than actually exists. There is also an artificial dichotomy created when one compares or contrasts "homosexuals" and "heterosexuals." In fact, sexual orientation exists across a spectrum and is not so easily divisible as may be implied, and the similarities between "homosexuals" and "heterosexuals" far outweigh the differences.

Psychotherapeutic Issues

Issues in psychotherapy with gay males and lesbian patients may be approached from either the standpoint of the patient or from the standpoint of the psychiatrist. Some common themes and issues such as homophobia and stereotyping may complicate treatment from both points of view.

From the standpoint of the psychiatrist, the initial contact with the gay patient can exert considerable influence on the course of therapy and may determine whether the patient will continue in treatment. The way in which the psychiatrist takes a history or asks questions of the patient may be particularly important and revealing. Certainly, the gay patient who is troubled by some issue will relate better to the psychiatrist who asks a question in such a way that a response involving a homosexual feeling or behavior can follow. For example, if sexual orientation has not been mentioned in an interview, the question "Are you currently dating anyone?" asked of a woman is preferable to initial questions such as "Are you currently dating any men?" or "Do you have a boyfriend?" A married male patient who indicates that he is having an affair with someone is not likely to be impressed by the psychiatrist who asks the patient to describe "her" when in fact the patient is referring to another male. Questions which assume that a patient is heterosexual are likely to be perceived by the patient as indicating that the psychiatrist is not knowledgeable or not perceptive or is unthinking, unskilled, or biased.

Words used as labels may reveal a bias on the part of the psychiatrist. Questions such as "How long have you had this problem?" or "How do you deal with the problem of homosexuality?" indicate that the psychiatrist views homosexuality as undesirable. Statements using a word such as *abnormal* as a label for an action or characteristic rather than a word such as *variation* also reveal the psychiatrist's bias.

Commonly used words such as *cause* or *etiology*, when used in reference to homosexuality, also suggest a bias insofar as these words ordinarily refer to disease states in medicine. For example, physicians speak of the etiology of cancer or mental illness but would not ordinarily speak of the etiology of naturally occurring characteristics such as blue eyes or white skin or left-handedness. It is important for psychiatrists to monitor their choices of words so that they do not unknowingly convey a subtle message that disparages the patient.

COUNTERTRANSFERENCE ISSUES

Psychiatrists must be aware of their own attitudes toward gay people and the effect these might have on their evaluation and treatment. A study of the effects of labeling an individual as homosexual in an experimental situation indicates that a male individual who was so labeled was seen as less clean, softer, more womanly, more tense, more yielding, more impulsive, less rugged, more passive, and quieter than the same individual not labeled as homosexual. (Karr 1978). If this finding were applicable to the psychiatrist's office, one might presume that the homosexual individual would be seen to exhibit more pathology or more negative characteristics than a similar heterosexual patient. The gay male who works out at the gym or who jogs to stay in shape may be seen as having a "problem" with narcissism or competition, while the heterosexual who engages in similar activity may be seen as having a positive sense of self-pride and achievement.

Such interpretations are examples of heterosexual bias in which heterosexuality is valued more highly and is favored over homosexuality. This bias results in certain actions being both devalued and at the same time falsely attributed to homosexuality. For example, positive achievements such as success in work may be interpreted as the result of a healthy or heterosexual side of an individual, while failures in work or relationships are attributed to a homosexual component. Heterosexual bias may also result in a prognosis for the homosexual patient being seen as less favorable than for a similar heterosexual patient. Therapeutic goals for the homosexual patient may then be unnecessarily attenuated or limited.

The homosexual patient may arouse anxiety and discomfort in the psychiatrist. One male patient related that a psychiatrist stated that the man that the patient was seeing was young enough to be the patient's son. The patient's own needless guilt was reinforced by this observation, although the patient believed that such an age difference in a heterosexual relationship would not be a cause of similar concern. The psychiatrist's discomfort with homosexual relationships in general may have led to a comment that presumably would not have been made about a heterosexual relationship involving the same age difference.

Issues presented by some gay patients, such as recreational sex or frequent sexual contact, may challenge the psychiatrist's value system. When the psychiatrist sees homosexual behavior per se as a sin or as morally wrong, it may be difficult, if not impossible, to be objective in dealing with psychological issues. If the psychiatrist holds a negative view of homosexuality, then strong consideration should be given to referring the gay patient to someone who views homosexuality in a more positive light.

THE COMING OUT PROCESS

The psychiatrist who works with gay men and lesbians should have a thorough acquaintance with the coming out process. Various models are available to describe this process, which may begin anytime from childhood to adult life (Cass 1979; Lee 1977; Troiden 1979). It can be arbitrarily separated into a series of stages which begin with a flicker of awareness that one is in some way different from other individuals. Those who progress completely through the entire sequence of gay identity formation come to acknowledge that they are gay or lesbian and proceed to integrate comfortably their sexual orientation into their self-concept.

Many gay individuals will experience some degree of discomfort as they begin to acknowledge their sexual orientation and are forced to deal with society's negative view of homosexuality, a view that they customarily incorporate to some degree. A major focus of therapy will often be this incorporated negative view of homosexuality. Therapy should aim both to reduce internalized homophobia and to assist the gay individual to develop a positive self-concept as the coming out process is completed.

Symptom formation in the gay patient may be related to an unsatisfactory resolution of the coming out process. Some gay individuals become fixated in very early conflict-ridden stages of this process, are imprisoned by their homophobia, and as a result lead unhappy and unproductive lives. The psychiatrist must recognize that this situation is not the inevitable fate of persons with a homosexual orientation but that it represents instead a failure to complete the coming out process successfully.

In relation to the coming out process, gay men and lesbians often believe and reiterate the myth that keeping their sexual orientation hidden will cause no problems for them. The psychiatrist sometimes reinforces this mistaken belief by asking the patient "Why do you want to 'flaunt' your homosexuality?" Although this may be a legitimate question in some cases, *flaunting* is often simply a negative label applied to any behavior that may result in some possible disclosure of sexual orientation. Whereas keeping one's sexual orientation a secret may be prudent and necessary under certain circumstances, being required to do so is likely to prevent individuals from feeling truly comfortable with themselves and with others. Keeping sexual orientation hidden usually necessitates remaining distant and aloof from potential friends, being secretive about one's life, and lying. Maintaining this secrecy requires a constant alertness and leaves a persistent underlying fear of the consequences of discovery. This fear necessarily results in a diminution in the quality of one's life that should not be overlooked and for which homosexuality per se should not be blamed. Being free to be open about sexual orientation can lead to a greater sense of comfort and satisfaction with life. Although psychiatrists do not necessarily need to encourage all of their gay patients to come out more openly, it should be kept in mind that homophobia on the part of either the patient or the psychiatrist may be a more important cause of keeping sexual orientation a secret than is the reality of the external environment.

PATIENT REACTIONS AND ATTITUDES

Gay male or lesbian patients will bring certain unique issues into the therapeutic situation. During the initial interview, many individuals will be uncomfortable revealing their sexual orientation because they are uncertain about the reception which such a revelation will receive. Many gay patients, because of previous experiences, are quite sensitive to any signs of rejection or bias and will readily note minor indications of discomfort on the part of the therapist. For example, one patient stated that he was sure that his psychiatrist was homophobic because when he discussed issues connected with homosexuality, the psychiatrist changed positions in his chair, his face reddened slightly, and there was some alteration in his voice.

Many gay patients will also automatically assume that the psychiatrist is heterosexual and expect the psychiatrist to respond to him or her as others have responded. Most gay patients are also aware of the historical attitude of psychiatry toward homosexuality. They may be mistrustful of the psychiatrist, an attitude that in turn will interfere with the development of a working relationship. Some patients may be immediately confrontational or challenging to determine the therapist's attitude about homosexuality. It is important that psychiatrists respond to inquiries about their views of homosexuality by openly acknowledging their beliefs. Then patients will be able to make an informed decision as to whether they wish to enter into treatment with a particular psychiatrist. Just as many black people would reject a psychiatrist who acknowledges that he or she feels that blacks are basically inferior to whites in some way, so many gay people will now reject a psychiatrist who views homosexuality negatively.

It is not uncommon for gay patients to describe dissatisfaction with prior treatment by a psychiatrist when the treatment was based on a model that stressed that homosexuality was pathological or when it involved an attempt to change sexual orientation. Already tormented by dissatisfaction with themselves, many of these individuals were overtly or covertly encouraged to give up essential sources of gratification, including friendships and relationships within the gay community as well as sexual contact with individuals to whom they were attracted. Such patients may speak of the wasted years of their lives, often with significant anger at their former therapists, whom they now regard as being uninformed, unknowledgeable, or biased. In addition, during their treatment some patients give a history of having developed or experienced an intensification of psychiatric symptoms such as depression, suicidal feelings, and social withdrawal. One can speculate that there may even be an increased risk of suicide when low self-esteem is made worse by treating the patient's sexual orientation as though it were pathological. Psychiatrists must be aware that overt or covert attempts to change sexual orientation are not simply innocuous procedures and that adverse side effects may be experienced by gay people when their treatment involves a model that considers homosexuality to be pathological (Brown 1976).

Dissatisfaction with prior treatment may make it difficult for some patients to feel comfortable with or to trust a new psychiatrist. These individuals may continue to test the psychiatrist's attitudes and may displace anger from the prior treatment setting to the new one. Such reactions will ordinarily be abated over time if the psychiatrist is consistently able to demonstrate an accepting and neutral attitude toward the patient's homosexuality.

STEREOTYPING

It is important that the psychiatrist not make any particular assumptions about a particular patient. Although virtually every psychiatrist would agree with such a statement in principle, until very recently the scientific and clinical literature has generally regarded homosexual individuals as if they were all identical and part of a homogeneous group. Psychodynamic explanations for the development of a homosexual orientation have often been put forward as if they apply to all homosexual men and women even though the conclusions have been derived from relatively small numbers of patients. Such incorrect generalizations are exemplified by the statement that "Every homosexual is an exquisite injustice collector, and consequently a psychic masochist" (Bergler 1956). This kind of statement is no different than statements of racial and religious stereotypes that have no foundation in research or science. In fact, gay men and lesbians are as diverse a group as are their heterosexual counterparts. Just as we do not assume that all blacks or all women are alike, we should not make similar assumptions about the characteristics of gay men and women. Some gay people are happy, some are not. Some function very well in work and love, some do not.

Psychiatrists should be particularly aware of the influence that cultural stereotypes have not only on themselves but on the gay patient. Among complaints that therapists hear from some gay patients are statements such as "All that gay men are interested in is sex," "No one is interested in a relationship," "No gays are really happy," and "No gay relationships last." It may be very easy for the psychiatrist who is unfamiliar with gay people and with the diversity of the gay community to assume incorrectly that the gay patient's observations are accurate. If the psychiatrist is unable to provide appropriate education or reality testing about the variety of individuals and life-styles associated with being gay, an unwitting collusion between the patient and psychiatrist will arise in which inaccurate negative stereotypes are reinforced and the patient's sense of self-esteem and comfort is lessened.

Negative stereotypes have been used and reinforced by some psychiatrists in attempts to make homosexuality ego-dystonic. For example, a psychiatrist asks "Can you see yourself as a sad aging homosexual?" (Hatterer 1970). In another instance, a patient repeats many of the stereotypes about a world presumably associated with homosexuality, and the psychiatrist replies "Everything you've observed is an accurate picture . . . " (Hatterer 1970). Rather than assisting patients to assess themselves realistically in relation to homosexuality, a negative bias is introduced, and the patient's options are limited rather than expanded. Unfortunately, many gay people may themselves believe in false stereotypes and will not be acquainted with or will fail to recognize the true diversity in the gay community. For such individuals, the psychiatrist should be able to serve as a source of education.

The characteristics of some gay individuals may appear to the psychiatrist to actually confirm stereotypes or theories about the pathology of homosexuality. Of course, in any large and diverse group of individuals there are likely to be a few individuals who fit virtually any stereotype that exists. Thus, one can find among gay men as well as among heterosexual men individuals who fit traditional gay male stereotypes. The existence of such individuals does not automatically prove that the stereotype or theory is accurate. For example, if one sees gay individuals who have difficulty forming close relationships, this should not result in an automatic conclusion that this is typical of gay people or that it confirms that homosexuality is pathological. Also, since it is not unusual for individuals to behave in ways that they are expected to behave, one might anticipate that some individuals in a group will come to behave in a manner that is consistent with the stereotype. A recent research study suggests that not only do some gay people behave in ways that they feel or that society feels are appropriate to them, but even their recall of past events may be distorted to fit the cultural bias (Ross 1980). A recent study of sexual preference from the Kinsey Institute concludes that homosexual patients may be taught to see or interpret their family backgrounds in ways that are consistent with the therapist's theoretical perspective (Bell et al. 1981). Therefore, the psychiatrist must be alert to the possibility of this retrospective distortion in working with gay men and lesbians and be cautious in fitting them into theoretical models.

ETHICS

A newly emerging area of concern in the treatment of gay men and women involves questions of ethics. These questions most frequently arise around the psychiatrist's role as a participant in legal or governmental actions where discrimination may take place based on sexual orientation. *The Principles of Medical Ethics with Annotations Especially Applicable to Psychiatry* (American Psychiatric Association 1981) was recently changed to read, "A psychiatrist should not be a party to any type of policy that excludes, segregates, or demeans the dignity of any patient because of . . . sexual orientation."

Psychiatrists are often asked to participate in legal or administrative proceedings that involve the issue of sexual orientation in some way. Examples of this include the right of a gay individual to exercise parental rights in child custody cases and the fitness of a gay individual to hold a particular job. Depending on the circumstances of each case, the participation of the psychiatrist may or may not be appropriate. It seems certain that the psychiatrist's role in these and similar situations will be scrutinized closely in the future. It is advisable that psychiatrists carefully assess the potential ramifications of their interventions with their gay patients to insure that harm is not done to the patient and to insure that such interventions do not violate the ethical guidelines of the profession.

SUMMARY

This chapter is offered as an overview of issues in the psychiatric treatment of gay men and lesbians. Many significant areas, such as the differences between gay men and lesbians and the effects of homophobia, require a much more detailed analysis than is possible here. It must be remembered that gay men and women will seek therapy for most of the same reasons that heterosexual men and women seek therapy. Too often, being gay is used by an individual or a psychiatrist as an excuse or explanation for what are actually psychological conflicts unrelated to being gay. For example, gay people do form lasting, meaningful, and intimate relationships. If a gay patient is unable to do so, the psychiatrist should not use this as evidence to persuade the individual that homosexuality is the source of this problem. Rather there should be an attempt to understand why this particular individual is having a problem with relationships just as there would be with any patient.

Homosexuality must not automatically be viewed as the root of all of the patient's problems. On the other hand, one must be sensitive to the significant impact that an awareness of being gay has on the individual who grows up in a society that so strongly condemns such an important manifestation of identity.

Ultimately the psychiatrist must be able to untangle these complex interactions. Working with the gay patient will require specialized knowledge and skills on the part of the psychiatrist, including a thorough understanding of the diversity of the gay community and the diversity of gay experiences. Most importantly, psychiatrists must be able to accord the same acceptance and respect to gay men and lesbians that they give to the rest of humanity.

References

Adelman MS: A comparison of professionally employed lesbians and heterosexual women on the MMPI. Arch Sex Behav 6:193–200, 1977

American Psychiatric Association: The Principles of Medical Ethics with Annotations Especially Applicable to Psychiatry, rev. ed. Washington, DC: American Psychiatric Association, 1981

Bell AP, Weinberg MS: Homosexualities: A Study of Diversity Among Men and Women. New York, Simon and Schuster, 1978

Bell AP, Weinberg MS, Hammersmith S: Sexual Preference, Bloomington. Indiana University Press, 1981

Bergler E: Homosexuality: Disease or Way of Life? New York, Collier Books, 1956

Brown H: Familiar Faces, Hidden Lives. New York, Harcourt, Brace, Jovanovich, 1976, pp 219–235

Cass VC: Homosexual identity formation: a theoretical model. J Homosex 4:219–235, 1979

Clark TR: Homosexuality and psychopathology in nonpatient males. Am J Psychoanal 35:163–168, 1975

Hart M, Roback H, Tittler B, et al.: Psychological adjustment of nonpatient homosexuals: critical review of the research literature. J Clin Psychiatry 39:604–608, 1978

Hatterer L: Changing Homosexuality in the Male. New York, McGraw-Hill, 1970

Karr RC: Homosexual labeling and the male role. Journal of Social Issues 34:74–83, 1978

Lee JA: Going public: a study in the sociology of homosexual liberation. J Homosex 3:49–78, 1977

Meredith RL, Reister RW: Psychotherapy, responsibility and homosexuality: clinical examination of socially deviant behavior. Professional Psychology 174:11, 174–193, 1980

Ross M: Retrospective distortion in homosexual research. Arch Sex Behav 9:523–531, 1980

Troiden RR: Becoming homosexual: a model of gay identity acquisition. Psychiatry 42:362–373 , 1979

5

Psychotherapy with Lesbian Couples: The Interrelationships of Individual Issues, Female Socialization, and the Social Context

Sallyann Roth, M.S.W.

5

Psychotherapy with Lesbian Couples: The Interrelationships of Individual Issues, Female Socialization, and the Social Context

The most significiant characteristics which distinguish lesbian couples as a clinical population arise from these few but crucial attributes: *(1)* a lesbian couple is comprised of two women; *(2)* the committed female couple is not a socially sanctioned family unit; and *(3)* full membership in such a couple requires the acceptance of a stigmatizable identity. Effective intervention in the couple relationships of lesbians requires that the therapist fully comprehend the reciprocities between the individual psychodynamics of the partners, the cultural patterning of female development, and the social position of the committed female pair.

The four major issues that have been presented by lesbian couples in early stages of treatment in my clinical practice are *(1)* problems of distance regulation and boundary maintenance between the two individuals and between the couple and those others who constitute their social world; *(2)* problems around sexual expression; *(3)* problems related to unequal access to

The author wishes to acknowledge that discussions with three colleagues—Richard Chasin, M.D., Ann Fleck Henderson, M.S.W., and Bianca Cody Murphy, Ed.D.—were particularly helpful in the formulation of many of the ideas presented in this chapter.

An earlier version of this chapter was presented at the Mental Health Service, University Health Services, Harvard University, on December 17, 1981.

material resources; and *(4)* problems arising from stage differences in coming out and development and management of individual lesbian identity. Of these issues, only the last is not also a major theme of beginning work with heterosexual couples. Although the first three themes are frequently present in distressed heterosexual and gay male couples, the way in which the themes are manifested in lesbian couples has a systematic regularity which seems related to the female composition of these couples.

As some coupling issues of lesbians vary from those of heterosexuals in a patterned way, so does breaking up. This chapter will address some of the special issues of both coupling and breaking up for lesbians.[1] (Note appears after the reference list.)

DISTANCE REGULATION AND BOUNDARY MAINTENANCE

Disagreement about distance regulation and boundary maintenance between partners is one of the most common problems in troubled couples (Karpel 1976; Feldman 1979). Indeed, in lesbian couples, whatever the stated presenting problem, the pain that precipitates the therapy contact can often be described as a too great distance between the partners' positions on the intimacy-distance continuum. Krestan and Bepko (1980, 277) describe "intense anxiety over any desire for separateness or autonomy within the relationship" as an invariant feature of lesbian couples in treatment. My clinical and supervisory experience leads me to use a broader description of the struggles to locate a mutually satisfying distance and mutually accepted methods of negotiating distance, a description which includes the anxiety and behaviors activated by too much distance as well as by too much closeness.

Although developmental psychology has traditionally attended centrally to male development, recent writers have attended to male-female differences in development and psychological style (Miller 1976; Chodorow 1978; Gilligan 1982; Henderson 1984). The unique female voice and vision elaborated by these writers include an orientation to the world of achievement and relationships from which one can predict the ways that the negotiation of contact and separateness could easily become problematic in a female couple. If both members of a couple are members of a societal group that has learned *(1)* to define self in relation to others (Chodorow 1978), *(2)* to define morality in terms of responsibility and care (Gilligan 1982), *(3)* to develop exceptional skills at noting the needs of others and to demonstrate this empathic stance even by experiencing the needs of others as their own (Chodorow 1978), and *(4)* to suppress aggressive and competitive desires to avoid hurting those for whom they care and to prevent the feared result of social isolation (Miller 1976), then that couple is at very high risk when successful coupling requires individuated self definition. If both members of a couple have been socialized so that the experience of being intimate with each other proffers "primary unity" (Chodorow 1978), so that each perceives the immediate possibility of experiencing the other as part of herself, intimate contact can easily raise frightening possibilities of merger, leaving that couple at high risk when successful coupling calls for intimate connection. The female couple presents, as does no other kind of couple, both the potential for fusion with its concomitant loss of self at the same moment that it proffers the potential for the most intense possible intimacy.

One member of a lesbian couple in treatment presented her version of the couple's problem this way: "We go from velcro—which is wonderful—to no contact at all, and then it seems like too much to go back. There is no middle ground. We don't seem to know how to do that." Indeed, ease of moving closer and then of moving back, experiencing deep connectedness and then solid separateness, are at best unfamiliar and awkward transitions, and at worst unavailable behaviors in the couples who seek treatment for problems of distance regulation. I have observed this phenomenon most often as a serious problem in couples who are isolated from the women's community.

The social surround for these couples brings its own pressure to bear on the issues of distance regulation and boundary maintenance. Krestan and Bepko (1980) have elaborately detailed the complex interaction between the positioning of lesbian couples in the larger heterosexual world and boundary-determining behavior within individual couples. They note, as does Toder (1979), that when a lesbian couple's attempts to define the boundaries around their relationship meet with no response or a response that is invalidating, the couple may need to rigidify its external boundary to insure couple integrity, thereby creating an increasingly closed system. Within the confines of any closed couple system, the individual boundaries are easily blurred. Other authors (Karpel 1976; Feldman 1979; Krestan and Bepko 1980) have described typical distancing strategies in response to the experienced dangers of fusion and overcloseness. These include *(1)* distancing by one partner or, in alternating sequence, by each; *(2)* open conflict (sometimes including physical violence); *(3)* triangling in of a third element (e.g., a romantic involvement with another person, increased involvement with a job); and *(4)* repeating cycles of alternating fusion and seeming unrelatedness.

Gilligan (1982, 63) has written that "we know ourselves as separate only insofar as we live in connection with others and we experience relationship only insofar as we differentiate other from self." The weight of female development adds to the boundary-invalidating or boundary-invading activities of the couple's larger environment and accentuates distance-regulation problems in lesbian couples.

[*Clinical example 1*]: A lesbian couple who bore the larger share of child care with one partner's children from a previous marriage were stressed by the children's father's behavior concerning weekends. When the couple planned a fishing trip for a weekend on which the children were to be with their father, he suggested that the children might enjoy going on the outing. When I asked the mother's partner if she thought the father would have behaved differently were she male, the mother stepped in and said, "Of course! He would be threatened if Joan were a man! He wouldn't want his children getting so attached to another man! This way, he just thinks they have two mothers and doesn't even think that there is any reason we might need to have a good time with just each other." While angered by what they experienced as an attempted boundary violation, both women were resigned to the father's behavior and used their shared anger to pull closer together.

The ways in which the boundaries around lesbian couples are affected by the heterosexual world are numerous. Some are unique to each couple, but others are regularly occurring events— and sometimes nonevents—that affect all lesbian couples.

The lesbian couple has no marker event to define the change in status from separate dating individuals or cohabiting couple to "married couple." The heterosexual ritual of marriage provides legitimization of boundaries, declares public expectation of the continuation of the dyadic unit into the future, and separates and differentiates young adults from their families of origin. The addition of children to the marital unit usually furthers the same process. There is community celebration around these events, which are seen as marking the passage from childhood to adult-hood. These events of marriage and becoming parents aid both the new couple's parents and the new couple themselves in recogniz-ing that those who were children (whatever their ages) have become fully adult and that new family-unit boundaries are now drawn, with three separate families defined where previously there were only two. Such societal validation, ceremonies of entry into adulthood, and support for coupling are largely unavailable to lesbian couples. On the contrary, the lesbian couple is invalidated by its usual invisibility in the larger heterosexual community. Even when it is quite visible, it is often disqualified as "not genuine," "not serious," "a stage," or pathological. It is also sometimes invalidated in the lesbian community where it may be seen as imitative of heterosexual culture.

Murphy (1982) notes that the lesbian couple may experience invalidation through rather direct forms of boundary invasion from the outside world. Closeted women are seen as single and asked for dates. Couples are given separate beds when visiting families. Partners are often not included in family holiday invita-tions and more importantly, may not have access to, or decision-making power for, each other in time of serious illness. Couples are not legally protected in mutual ownership of property unless they take legal steps to establish joint ownership.

[*Clinical example 2*]: One couple conversed quietly and pleasantly about trouble they had in making decisions about important life events. They seemed to be caring and attentive to each other, each stating concerns while the other listened carefully and asked penetrating but kind questions. Observing their being so attentive to each other, I did not understand that they were fighting until I noticed that they never achieved resolution on any point but merely alternated taking the tenderly interested and care-taking position. Curiously, although one of them was always in the position of attending carefully, neither one experienced the other as close. Differences were never openly stated, nor were strong statements made about what each needed for herself.

Initial work with this couple consisted of clarifying the differentiated positions of each, interrupting and calling attention to the care taking and avoidance of self-declaring statements, and framing the seemingly caring stances toward each other as a lack of respect each had for the other's ability to protect and care for herself, a behavior that actually diminished each partner in turn. In this construction, to continue to behave as a caretaker would have been for either woman a demonstration of lack of caring.

Within a few weeks, the couple were openly fighting and fairly well able to carry on toward resolution of differences without much further intervention. I regarded this intervention as an interruption of a disabling sequence which was the almost inevitable result of female socialization.

Hall (1978) describes work with a similar couple, saying she instructed members of the couple to face each other and use the words "I disagree" several times in the first interview.

[*Clinical example 3*]: Another couple came to my office at the point of deciding whether or not to move in together. Two agendas seemed prominent. First, they were seeking witness as well as counsel to their coming together as a more committed couple. With regard to this agenda, my role was simply defined. I had only to see and hear them and to demonstrate the belief that their committed coupling was a viable choice. Second, they feared that living in the same physical space, they would not be able to negotiate private space. I saw this fear as both real and metaphorical, and we spent several sessions addressing this multileveled issue.

The exploration of society's influence on female development in areas affecting boundary maintenance and distance regulation as it applies to lesbian couples is not a trivial exercise. In the past, it was common for clinicians to see the behaviors associated with

these difficulities in lesbian dyads as evidence of arrested psychological development associated with rather serious pathology.
Although some members of some lesbian couples may in fact
suffer such developmental arrest, it would be an error to assume
that coupling difficulties around boundary maintenance and
distance regulation of the sort I have described are necessarily
indicators of such problems.

PROBLEMS OF SEXUAL EXPRESSION IN LESBIAN COUPLES

Lesbians, being women, "have their share of sexual problems...
similar to the general [female] population. Lesbians may have
primary or more often secondary sexual dysfunction, when
relationship problems are expressed in the sexual realm"
(Loewenstein 1980, 35). Loewenstein (1980) reports that fear of
being touched, sexual inhibitions, and highly ritualized lovemaking patterns are sometimes associated with remaining conflicts about lesbian identity. This section will address other sexual
problems which are particularly related to the committed female
couple, because numerous other writers address the sexual issues
of women in general and because the three issues mentioned by
Loewenstein are better viewed and dealt with as identity issues
than as sexual ones. The sexual problems addressed in this section
therefore are limited to monogamy versus nonmonogamy, heterosexual fantasies and behavior, and infrequency of genital sexual
contact.

Monogamy Versus Nonmonogamy

Many lesbians live in monogamous relationships quite akin to
traditional marriages, often including children of one or both
partners from a prior heterosexual marriage or liaison, children by
adoption, or children conceived through artificial insemination. A
substantial group of politically involved lesbians have committed
themselves intellectually and in practice to opposing this form of
coupling, asserting that it mimics that dominant heterosexual

social form with all of its institutionalized inequalities and exploitation and is thereby demeaning and destructive to women. Women's socialization, however, frequently makes it difficult for lesbians to live up to these "liberated" ideals (Hall 1978; Toder 1979; Loewenstein 1980; Blumstein and Schwartz 1983).

According to Blumstein and Schwartz (1983, 301),

> Women do not do well with outside involvements. Lesbians live in a world that espouses two sets of contradictory values. One ideology rejects monogamy because it is a symbol of men's traditional control of women. Another prizes traditional 'female virtues' and rejects 'male values.' Not surprisingly, therefore, lesbians prefer sex to take place in a context of warmth, affection, and respect, not to be a purely physical experience. It is easy to understand why they commit themselves ideologically to sexual freedom but find it difficult to put into practice. Women are neither instructed nor experienced in the art of casual sex; having sex with someome requires liking or loving the other person. Outside sex, if it occurs, is usually romantic, not casual, and frequently provokes a crisis of trust between the two women in the relationship. Lesbian couples can survive nonmonogamy, expecially if it happens in a solid relationship, but rarely does it become part of their lives.

Two clinical examples illustrate some problems lesbian couples have regarding monogamy and nonmonogamy.

[*Clinical example 4*]: One professional lesbian couple reported that they had moved from a small rural city with a large radical feminist population after eight years of residence there because they experienced the constant pressure to be nonmonogamous as potentially destructive to their relationship. They had decided several years earlier that they would not admit their monogamy within the social/political community for fear that they would be ostracized and socially isolated. For some years this couple had engaged in a double deception. Their lesbian friends thought that each of them had affairs. Their parents thought that they were roommates. The once uncomfortable untruths became intolerable when they decided to add a child to their family.

[*Clinical example 5*]: A young lesbian couple came to therapy because one member of the couple wanted to open the sexual boundaries of the relationship. She was attracted to another woman and wanted her partner, who was threatened by the proposal, to approve of her entering into a relationship with the other woman. Both members of the couple quickly understood that this potential extra-couple liaison was of emotional as well as physical import and that they needed to address their mutual dissatisfactions in the present relationship. Although the "affair" was proposed in political terms, in this particular case it reflected an unexpressed rupture in the emotional bond between the two women. The affair did not occur and the relationship broke up.

Heterosexual Fantasies and Behaviors

Many lesbians are privately distressed by sexual feelings, fantasies, and dreams about men, and they experience their awareness of these interests as threatening to their usually hard-won lesbian identity and membership in the lesbian subculture. There is no more justification to consider these thoughts and feelings, even when acted upon occasionally, as a demonstration of the lesbian's "basic heterosexuality" than there is to consider the sometime homosexual fantasy or behavior of a heterosexual person as a demonstration of his or her "basic homosexuality." Since the lesbian community largely looks with disfavor upon these heterosexual interests and behaviors, and with even greater disfavor upon bisexuality, lesbians in the treatment context are often tremendously relieved to be able to speak of them at all; and they are doubly relieved, though often uncomfortable at first, to speak of them with their partners.

Toder (1978, 111) notes that there is a taboo in the lesbian community against talking about these experiences and that "many lesbians assume that other lesbians never have them and literally panic when they have a sexual fantasy or dream that includes men." It might be useful to term this reaction *heterophobia* to point out that it has a parallel in the well known homophobia of heterosexual life and to indicate that in the lesbian community, heterosexuality is often stigmatized.

For the heterosexual therapist, the exploration of these issues is a delicate matter because lesbian women are ever alert for signs that the therapist disapproves of or does not support their life-styles and object choice and may suspect the therapist's reason for raising these issues. It may, in fact, not be possible for some lesbians to discuss these issues in such a context. In some cases, if the heterosexual therapist demonstrates a willingness for the clients to discuss these matters in consultation with a self-identified lesbian therapist, this attitude of openness may render such a consultation unnecessary. Although the sexual orientation of the therapist may make an important difference in dealing with this topic, the therapist's values and attitudes and the communication of them to the clients are far more significant.

Intolerance of bisexuality or of inconsistent object choice is perhaps even greater in the lesbian than in the heterosexual community. Thus those many women who experience themselves as having the potential for significant relationships with women and with men often feel lonely and trapped with their feelings and confusions. These are frequently named in therapy in times of deepening commitment within the couple, when the member experiencing them is addressing her own grief over the loss of heterosexual privilege, the possibility of bearing a child who is biologically related to both parents, and sometimes, sexual relations with men.

Infrequency of Genital Sexual Contact

Although lesbian couples generally report substantial satisfaction with the quality of their sex life (Bell and Weinberg 1978; Toder 1978, 1978; Blumstein and Schwartz 1983), it is an emerging truth that lesbians have genital sex less frequently than do married heterosexual couples, cohabiting heterosexual couples, or gay male couples. It is also becoming evident that infrequency of, and unequal desire for, genital sex are the primary sexual complaints even in nonclinical populations of lesbian couples (Toder 1978; Tanner 1978; Blumstein and Schwartz 1983). Although I initially believed that infrequent genital sex was an expectable outgrowth of the distance-regulation difficulties explicated earlier in this chapter, I have come to see that as a far too limiting vision.

A fuller view includes, yet again, aspects of female socialization that might easily be factors in decreasing the quantity of sexual contacts between partners, as well as the ways in which the social surround of lesbian couples has a limiting effect on expression of sexuality. Women in our culture have been taught that their own sexuality is to be inhibited and repressed and have learned to express their sexuality most often in terms of the "other's" needs and wishes, being less attuned to the messages of their own body (Rubin 1976; Henderson 1984). Female training in repression of one's own sexuality includes, of course, an injunction against being assertive or initiating sex. Predictably, when two people are paired who share such an injunction, sexual encounters are minimal until efforts are made to develop a different stance through education and through open exploration of those events that precede acts of holding back when either wishes to approach the other.

Blumstein and Schwartz (1983, 303) point out that

[heterosexual] couples who share sexual privileges [of initiation and refusal]—and couples where the male assumes all of the responsibility—can have a satisfying sex life. The snag in heterosexual relationships occurs when the couple assigns sexual responsibilities in ways that go against each sex's prior training. If women take most of the initiative and men are sexually coy, then both frequency and satisfaction suffer.

The authors recognize the special dilemma for female couples:

Lesbians are caught betwixt and between. Neither partner is fully comfortable with sexual aggressiveness nor with the belief that one partner ought to dominate. If each woman could adopt an active role in sexual matters then their activity would be greater. If one woman could be assigned the active role without provoking the other's resentment, sexual frequency would increase. But one or the other strategy would have to be agreed upon (Blumstein and Schwartz 1983, 303).

Such an agreement in itself would not necessarily solve this difficulty, because when one person initiates often, she is certain to be turned down some of the time. Men are used to this; they accept as truth that women have less frequent interest in sex than they do and generally perceive a "no" as indication of this difference between them. Women, on the other hand, are far more likely to think that a negative response to a sexual initiative is a rejection of them, not of the sexual act (Blumstein and Schwartz 1983), and to experience the anxiety associated with emotional cut-off. This, too, is a factor in diminishing numbers of approaches women make to their partners. In addition, the impact of women's need to be in good emotional contact with their partners before freely engaging in genital sex must not be minimized (Rubin 1976; Henderson 1984). In fact, this particularly female stance has clashed painfully with men's need to reconnect through sex when there are relationship difficulties in heterosexual couples (Rubin 1976). What this means for lesbian couples, however, is that the sexual relationship is substantially more vulnerable to emotional disharmony between its members than is the sexual relationship of heterosexual partners.

For many lesbian women, lesbian sexuality is a learned response and for some of them it is hard won. Many lesbians today make their partner choice on the basis of emotional preference and assume that they can develop their interest in lesbian sexuality (Henderson 1979). Others feel immediately physically attracted and responsive to women, but are so imbued with cultural proscriptions against such contact that they have to work to overcome these barriers. Henderson (1979, 178) reports a young lesbian's comment, "It's amazing how many inhibitions I have against making love with a woman. It's the training. The attraction is there, but it's hard to do." The difficulties of learning to be comfortable with lesbian sexuality in a culture that is disapproving of such sexual expression have been partially lessened by the publication of several informed and explicit books that serve to desensitize the subject, but these are, on the whole, available only to an urban and educated lesbian population.

The social context is also relevant in the sexual arena. There is a discontinuity between traveling in the outside world, where any overt show of sexually tinged affection may put a lesbian couple at serious risk, and arriving home, where all levels of contact are fine. The warming-up process may thus be significantly attenuated or interrupted by the social context in which it occurs.

Given the psychological and sociological variables just described, it is not surprising that some lesbian couples often go without genital sex for considerable lengths of time. The greater the duration of these times, the more mutually avoidant of sex the partners become. Clinical requests for help with this issue of too little genital sex frequently come when couples have reached such an impasse. Often the topic is broached by requests for normative information about the sexual frequency of other lesbians. When I have broadened the discussion and shared with lesbian clients information about socialization as it relates to frequency, they have almost uniformly expressed deep interest and relief. The information-giving portion of these sessions is commonly a ground-breaking prerequisite for detailed exploration of the partners' experiences around genital sexual activity and inactivity.

Occasionally the infrequency itself is not experienced as a problem, but as something the couple's members *think* they should worry about. More often, infrequency is experienced by one partner as a serious problem and has been understood as a discrepancy in desire, one which has been played out so many times with so much pain that the partner defined in the couple as the more desirous one has withdrawn all approaches. Although plans for treatment are as numerous as couples in therapy and may be tied to any unsettled issue within the couple relationships, methods of interrupting recurring sequences of sexual apprehension are more generalizable.

Behavioral prescriptions—involving stimulation of behaviors belonging to a time before this problem became a disabling preoccupation, involving the equal sharing of present actions, introducing novelty or playfulness, or encouraging restraint from genital sex—have been variously effective. These and other methods of interrupting disabling sequences resemble those used with heterosexual couples at similar impasses (Masters and Johnson 1970; Kaplan 1979).

Although this section has addressed the issue of infrequency of genital contact in lesbian couples, it is important to note that lesbians as a group "prize nongenital physical contact—cuddling, touching, hugging—probably more than other couples do. But more important, they are much more likely to consider these activities as ends in themselves, rather than as foreplay leading to genital sex" (Blumstein and Schwartz 1983, 197). Blumstein and Schwartz think that the need for nongenital lovemaking is probably equal among lesbian and heterosexual women, but heterosexual women make an adaptation to male sexuality, accepting the snuggling and touching as foreplay, a precursor to coitus, even when they might prefer only nongenital pleasuring.

STRESS RELATED TO UNEQUAL ACCESS TO RESOURCES

Women who came out after the women's movement began usually strive for the ideal of independence and autonomy within an egalitarian relationship. The strain they experience in their strivings is analogous to that of heterosexual partners who are working to develop relationships of equality and autonomy in a context that has few models for such behaviors and beliefs. Here, female couples may actually have an advantage, as women's culture has historically assumed a model of collaboration among women, and the women's community is consistently supportive of such values and efforts.

Since lesbian women frequently meet in settings where the commonality is sexual orientation and not social class, education, or work, they often connect with women whose financial status and social mobility are substantially different from their own. It is a truism in heterosexual society that there are major differences in income between partners. In fact, women are generally raised to believe that they will marry men who will either support them or at least have greater earning power and professional status than they. Why then might this inequality be problematic in a different way for lesbian couples? It is sometimes difficult for the partner who earns more because she daily faces the discrepancy between her socialization to depend on a provider and the reality of her being more of provider than her partner. It is more often difficult for both women because it violates the philosophical and political ideal of equality, an ideal endorsed by the lesbian community and one that offers the couple exemption from the high price traditionally paid by heterosexual partners for the woman's financial dependence and status sharing.

Lesbian couples develop extraordinarily creative financial arrangements to avoid power imbalances in financial decision making and planning and to maintain a sense of interdependence without losing independence. It is common to keep money separate for the early years of the relationship and to keep detailed accounts of exactly who has spent how much for what, with attempts made to keep contributions for living expenses exactly equal. Often large "debts" are built up, debts that may never be paid but that allow the illusion or promise of equal contribution even as the actual practice is clearly quite different. Sometimes the partner who "owes" feels burdened by the debt; she does not believe it is unfair to owe it, in fact wants desperately to pay it, but feels uncomfortable permitting the higher-income partner to continue paying more. Thus, a lower-income woman might be uncomfortable and upset should her higher-income partner purchase something "extra" for them both such as a vacation, new appliance, or restaurant dinner, while the higher-income woman may resent not having the freedom to use her additional earnings to enhance their lives.

The practice of keeping books fairly balanced and money quite separate usually forms the pattern of the early years, although there are variations. A common variation on the fifty-fifty arrangement is that of keeping contributions to joint expenses proportional to the incomes of each partner. Toder (1979) sees the separation of finances as destructive to lesbian couples and suggests that an earlier mingling of resources might encourage couples to work harder at their relationship during rough times. Blumstein and Schwartz (1983) report that merging of money takes place gradually and is usually related to the process of deepening commitment. They notice that pooling money is a statement of trust that the partners now believe their relationship is going to last. Some couples name each other as beneficiaries in wills or insurance policies as a prestage to the actual mingling of finances.

In my practice during the last few years, five lesbian couples have come for treatment who reported that their homes were owned by only one partner while both contributed equal money and labor for the upkeep. In each instance, it was as they moved into a position of greater trust and began to pool their resources in other ways that this remaining inequality became burdensome. Since the mingling of resources requires more mutuality in concrete decisions of daily living and life planning, there is an increase in the potential for conflict once money and property are pooled (Blumstein and Schwartz 1983). Lesbian couples may not attempt this pooling until they believe that their relationship can handle the increased conflict. Arrangements for handling the sharing of resources in a relationship of equality while having different income levels do not appear to be widely discussed. Thus, couples usually must struggle quite independently with this problem. Additionally, they may lack information about ways to pool resources that allow both for sharing and for financial protection. Here legal and financial consultants are essential, and the therapist cannot take their place. Of course, financial sharing on any but the smallest scale also involves possible exposure in the outside world. After one woman added her partner's name to the deed for her house, she became anxious when mortgage statements arrived in the mail addressed to both of them.

Although difficulties over allocation of money are frequently both real and metaphorical expressions of power struggles in heterosexual and gay male relationships, the symbolic and real importance of these struggles for lesbians is usually the avoidance of dependence and the establishment of equality (Blumstein and Schwartz 1983).

STAGE DIFFERENCES IN COMING OUT AND DEVELOPMENT OF INDIVIDUAL LESBIAN IDENTITY

Many women engage in deep emotional and sexual relationships with other women, sometimes for long periods of time, without construing their involvements to mean that they are lesbian

(Ponse 1978). Thus it is possible that a woman who is in a couple relationship with another woman may not have self-identified as a lesbian at all or may not have fully embraced a lesbian identity with all of its complexities. The implications of this are profound.

When members of a female couple who have not defined themselves as lesbian are deepening their commitment to one another, identity issues that have been kept at a distance will enter the heart of the relationship. In couples in which the partners are moving on different time schedules through the stages of accepting a lesbian identity and coming out, the slower movement of one member may be experienced by the other as threatening to the relationship. The faster movement of one partner may be experienced by the other as threatening to her own sense of self and her safety from stigma and ostracism. It is not at all unusual for the behavioral manifestations of these stage differences to be interpreted within the couple as acts of alienation, assault, or abandonment. For these reasons, female couples commonly seek therapy in periods of forward movement when they are mutually deepening their relationship and identity issues are stirred up or when one partner is demonstrating greater comfort with her lesbian identity.

Whether the stress presented is around issues of coming out or of more fully embracing a lesbian identity, the therapist's task is, at first, to frame the problem so that the partners develop a meta-position from which to view it, one which does not stimulate accusatory and defensive behavior.

[*Clinical example 6*]: A woman whose love involvements had been almost entirely with women for 20 years found herself grieving during the early stages of a relationship which she recognized carried with it the possibility of lifelong commitment. She was distressed not only by her sad feelings, but by the inexplicable juxtaposition of these feelings with the elation of being in love. She was relieved of the latter distress, though still quite pained, when she realized she was giving up two incompatible secret beliefs (so secret that even she had been barely aware of them). The first was the belief that she would someday have a partner who would also be welcomed and accepted as kin by her family. The second was the belief (an impossible one, given her lifestyle) that she would, without loss, eventually achieve an identity that was continuous through all the contexts of her life. In these beliefs, she had hoped to put an end to the deception of passing as heterosexual at work and with family and to gain an intimacy with family and coworkers which was impossible while she kept her relationships hidden. She had hoped she could achieve this limited coming out without rupturing important relationships in her larger world. Once she was involved in the complex grieving process that goes on at this stage of solidifying lesbian identity, even she was able to see that her choices of unsatisfactory prior partners had in part been predicated on avoiding this difficult self-confrontation.

Her lover, being at a different stage in this process, was bewildered and hurt by expressions of confusion and deep sadness where she had expected only excitement and pleasure. She was helped to recall her own grief work around the identity shift from heterosexual to lesbian and to understand that the withdrawal and sadness of her partner indicated not abandonment, but love and promise for the future.

[*Clinical example* 7]: One partner's self-acceptance as a lesbian took the form of increasing her visibility as a representative of the lesbian community, a stance which was taken as a direct attack by her partner, a professional woman who believed that her entire career and livelihood would be destroyed should she be exposed. Discussion had to shift from accusations of destructive intent and mutual covert power plays to the uncomfortable realization that these two people simply had to accept as life problems an unjust social reality and a significant difference between them as individuals, both of which problems had serious implications for their future as a couple and as individuals. They were blaming each other and were focused solely on the different adjustments each had made to society, instead of identifying the larger social system as the source in their dilemma.

The crucial time for self-confrontation about lesbian identity is the time of relationship commitment, a situation easily understandable in a culture where women make their fundamental definitions of self through relationship (Chodorow 1978). The therapeutic dilemma in cases like these is that identity conflicts may be presented in the service of avoiding commitment to relationship, and the fear of commitment to relationship may be presented as avoidance of commitment to a lesbian identity with its stigma and concomitant grief process. The therapeutic task is to openly and fully explore both sides of the dilemma with an educated recognition of potential costs and benefits for each woman of fully embracing a lesbian identity. Lesbian and gay therapists may have more investment in seeing the benefits than the costs, and heterosexual therapists greater investment in seeing the costs than the benefits. Therapists of all persuasions are likely to overcompensate for any position they are not entirely comfortable with and may also feel stuck with their client in the chicken-and-egg problem of relationship commitment and acceptance of lesbian identity.

BREAKING UP

Lesbian women sometimes hold onto their relationships well past the point when they seem workable to them (Hall 1978). There are doubtless many reasons for this holding on. In my clinical practice, the most common reason is that women experience the act of initiating a breakup as a violation of the female ethic of care and a failure to obey the societal injunction to women to work on and nurture relationships. Less common, but recurring, reasons include (1) angry rebellion against the heterosexual world's view that homosexual relationships do not last and fear that the break up of a relationship is evidence that the dominant society's vision is accurate, and (2) recognition of the difficulty of finding a suitable partner in a limited and largely invisible population.

When a couple comes to therapy on the verge of breaking up, yet is unable to do so, the therapist must repeatedly raise the possibility of the couple's ending the relationship or continuing into the future just as they are. It may take some time for at least one partner to fully accept the need to end the relationship and take definitive action. Since often in lesbian couples a woman's mate is also her best friend, the loss is initially a multiple one. It is characteristic in the lesbian community for former lovers to become part of each other's continuing friendship network after the immediate pain of the breakup subsides and one or both are reconnected with other partners (Roth and Murphy 1978; Tanner 1978; Krestan and Bepko 1980). Although this practice has arisen, at least in part, from the small size and closed nature of the lesbian community, it usually serves women well, providing a sense of continuity and connection. Krestan and Bepko (1980) have emphasized the convenient possibilities for triangulation of former lovers into new relationships provided by this custom. Although I have sometimes observed such triangulation, I have more often witnessed the transformation of former lovers into helpful long-term "family friends."

If a couple have been together for some time and have pooled their money or made major joint purchases such as a house or vacation property or if they co-own a business, the therapist may be called upon to help negotiate a property distribution at the time of breakup. The partners' legal protection can only be as extensive as the specific contracts they have made along the way, and a neutral outsider may be needed to mediate. The symbolic value of this act of mediation may be as great as its pragmatic value because it is a witnessed ritual providing closure on the partners' lives together.

CONCLUSION

The patterned expression of four of the themes discussed above in lesbian couples varies with systematic regularity from their expression in heterosexual couples. Yet each lesbian couple also develops unique patterns related to these themes which derive from the individual psychology of both women and the nature of their connection with each other.

> [*Clinical example 8*]: The six years during which Alice and Pamela had lived together coincided with the passing through adolescence of five of their six children. Neither the children nor any of Alice and Pamela's co-workers had been told the nature of the women's relationship. At the time the couple came for therapy, the last of their children had just entered adolescence. Alice had just added Pamela's name to the deed of the house in which they all lived and which Alice had acquired as part of a divorce settlement. Alice regarded her act as a formal goodbye to the "ghosts" of her heterosexual past and her particular marriage, as well as the achievement of a further stage in her commitment to Pamela and acceptance of her lesbian identity. During this same period of time Pamela became impatient with Alice's lesser and diminishing interest in sexual activity and greater

emotional distance. Alice's verbalized temptation to come out to some of her coworkers verged on realization, leaving Pamela in a state of anxiety and upset. When their arguments about these things and the periods of emotional distance increased, they initiated therapy. Although there was a substantial discrepancy in their incomes, they split the therapy fee exactly in half.

Alice's characteristic stance in the world and in the couple was one of hope and goodwill persistently inhibited by fear of impending doom, anger, and abandonment. She related this stance to a regularly occurring interaction with her mother in which the mother seemed warm and accepting at one moment, then later was hostile and attacking. Alice was always waiting for the unpredictable and unjust hostile attack.

Pamela's characteristic stance in the world and in the couple was one of trying to make things better. She regarded any sign of unhappiness in her partner as a response to her own failure to fix things. She related this to a regularly occurring interaction with her mother in which the mother was severely depressed and nonfunctional. Pamela tried to make her feel better by caring for younger siblings, keeping them quiet, making up entertaining stories and songs, cooking, and by age eleven, generally taking over the household. Pamela constantly scanned her interpersonal field for signals that others, especially Alice, were drifting away and that she would be alone with her despairing feelings of not being able to "make it right."

Alice and Pamela requested to work on issues of "how we negotiate distance and closeness, of what we bring [to the relationship] that brings more distance than closeness," of time and space negotiations, of Alice's tentative coming out behavior triggering anxiety attacks in Pamela, and of disagreements about sex. Although it was clear that money was scarce in their household, it never became a subject of therapy, and the material reported here on the ways that unequal earnings affected their relationship was only revealed in a follow-up interview.

Distance Regulation and Boundary Maintenance. For Alice, trouble at transitions between distance and closeness included *(1)* feeling hopeful and joyous about coming home, then turning off her hope before arriving, *(2)* wanting space and time alone and wanting to get them without having to negotiate, and *(3)* wanting to be able to be close and talk when something bothered her and to have Pamela "just listen." To address the first problem, she needed to stop anticipating a repeat of interaction with her mother. To address the second, she needed to brave risking Pamela's displeasure by making direct statements about what she wanted. To address the third, Pamela had to stop trying to "make it all better."

For Pamela, trouble at transitions from closeness to distance and back again was characterized by confusion and mystery. Her fantasy of an easy transition was that she and Alice would be making love, Pamela would hug Alice and remind her, "I'd love to stay longer, but I have a plane to catch and the taxi is waiting." Successful separations for Pamela had to be anticipated, had to include acknowledgment that distance was regrettable, and had to overtly honor the intimacy that was being left. Successful separations also had to include mutual acknowledgment that Pamela's leaving was not hurting Alice and that Alice's leaving was not a response to Pamela's "not being good enough."

In separations during difficult times, when Alice and Pamela could not manage satisfactory negotiation of distance, Pamela might feel inadequate and try harder to come closer. Alice, who might have withdrawn only to put up her feet and balance her checkbook, would be mystified and panicked by Pamela's insistent attention to relationship when Alice did not see a problem. Alice would then feel that she was being unjustly and unpredictably attacked. She would withdraw further and might even express annoyance and irritability at the "constant intrusions" of Pamela. This sequence recycled numerous times, with its beginning point being variously identified by the women as Pamela's or Alice's.

Problems of Sexual Expression. Alice, who was the more reluctant and restrained partner in sexual activity, said that she feared that if she really engaged in sex wholeheartedly and frequently, there might be an "unpleasant surprise." She might discover later that even though Pamela and she seemed to be having a wonderful experience at the time, Pamela might change her mind later and say that it had not been good enough.

Coming Out. Pamela feared that if she came out to people she cared about, they might be upset and she would feel she had to make them feel better. She also knew that she was powerless to take on and cure the world's homophobia and did not want to feel that inadequacy. Alice feared that people would respond well to her coming out first and then be angry or abandoning later. She feared that she would learn she could not trust in the future those whom she had trusted in the past.

Unequal Access to Material Resources. Alice, who earned less than Pamela, was angry and frightened whenever Pamela spent money on "extras" for which she could not contribute equally. She feared that the inequality would unbalance their relationship. She also feared that this spending would place them in a situation where their family might be in unpredictable danger. Pamela was bewildered because Alice would not countenance her spending money to make their lives easier and was not cheered by her gifts.

Although this case example focuses on the highly personal constructs each partner brought to the couple as they affected coupling difficulties, the work of therapy did not solely explore the intertwining of these individual issues. These were consistently addressed as connected to and partially shaped by the larger social context of the heterosexual and lesbian communities and the nature of female sex-role development.

Effective therapy with lesbian couples requires that the therapist be skilled at seeing the interrelationships between individual, couple, and social themes. Attempts to normalize lesbian couples by addressing themes only as unique and personal ignore the complex reverberations of female socialization and societal homophobia. Attempts to relate problems of lesbian coupling merely to the individual's or the couple's political position within the dominant society ignore the uniquely personal aspects of each couple. Alternatively, a vision is required that encompasses all these multileveled themes and that comprehends their many complex and often subtle reciprocities.

References

Bell AP, Weinberg MS: Homosexualities: A Study of Diversity Among Men and Women. New York, Simon and Schuster, 1978

Blumstein P, Schwartz P: American Couples. New York, William Morrow, 1983

Chodorow N: The Reproduction of Mothering: Psychoanalysis and the Sociology of Gender. Berkeley, University of California Press, 1978

deMonteflores C, Schultz S: Coming out: similarities and differences for lesbians and gays. Journal of Social Issues 34:59–72, 1978

Feldman LTS: Marital conflict and marital intimacy: an integrative psychodynamic-behavioral-systemic model. Fam Process 18:69–78, 1979

Gilligan C: In a Different Voice: Psychological Theory and Women's Development. Cambridge, Harvard University Press, 1982

Hall M: Lesbian families: cultural and clinical issues. Social Work 23:380–385, 1978

Henderson AF: College age lesbianism as a developmental phenomenon. Journal of the American College Health Association 28:176–178, 1979

Henderson AF: Homosexuality in the college years: developmental differences between men and women. Journal of the American College Health Association (in press)

Kaplan HS: Disorders of Sexual Desire and Other New Concepts and Techniques in Sex Therapy. New York, Brunner/Mazel, 1979

Karpel M: Individuation: from fusion to dialogue. Fam Process 15:65–82, 1976

Krestan J, Bepko C: The problem of fusion in the lesbian relationship. Fam Process 3:19–24, 1980

Loewenstein S: Understanding lesbian women. Social Casework 61:29–38, 1980

Masters WH, Johnson VE: Human Sexual Inadequacy. Boston, Little Brown and Co, 1970

Miller JB: Toward a New Psychology of Women. Boston, Beacon Press, 1976

Moses AE: Identity Management in Lesbian Women. New York, Praeger, 1978

Murphy BC: Intergenerational contact and the impact of parental attitudes on lesbian and married couples: a comparative study. Unpublished doctoral dissertation, Boston University School of Education, Boston, 1982

Ponse B: Identities in the Lesbian World: The Social Construction of Self. Westport, Conn., Greenwood Press, 1978

Riddle DI, Song B: Psychotherapy with lesbians. Journal of Social Issues 34:84–100, 1978

Roth S, Murphy BC: The importance of "loss" as a clinical issue with lesbian couples. Presented at Third Annual New England Feminist Therapy Conference, Boston, 1978

Rubin LB: Worlds of Pain: Life in the Working Class Family. New York, Basic Books, 1976

Tanner D: The Lesbian Couple. Lexington, Mass., Lexington Books, 1978

Toder N: Sexual problems of lesbians, in Our Right to Love: A Lesbian Resource Book. Edited by Vida G. Englewood Cliffs, NJ, Prentice-Hall, 1978

Toder N: Lesbian couples: special issues, in Positively Gay. Edited by Berzon B, Leighton R. Millbrae, Calif., Celestial Arts, 1979

Vida G (ed): Our Right to Love: A Lesbian Resource Book. Englewood Cliffs, NJ, Prentice-Hall, 1978

Note

[1]Although the group of issues discussed in this chapter is by no means exhaustive, it represents those of greatest importance among those lesbian couples in my clinical practice. They are predominantly white, middle class, and either under forty or, if older, consist of women who became coupled with other women well after the women's movement began. Some of these issues would look quite different if nonwhite women and women who came out in isolation at a time of much greater oppression were included in this clinical sample.

Psychotherapy for Male Couples: An Application of Staging Theory

David P. McWhirter, M.D.
Andrew M. Mattison, M.S.W., Ph.D.

6

Psychotherapy for Male Couples: An Application of Staging Theory

Psychotherapy for relationships has been an important interest of ours for more than 10 years. Our particular focus on male couples started sometime in 1973 when we began psychotherapy with gay men in and out of relationships. Looking for some answers to questions that these patients were asking about other men in relationships, we went to the literature and found nothing useful. There was some research, mostly psychoanalytic in orientation, which focused on the psychopathology of homosexuality and the consequent limitations of and obstacles to relationship formation. Saghir and Robins (1973) had just published studies about gay people stressing many short-term relationships. Even so, there was no information answering the questions our patients were asking such as, How do other men live their daily lives together? How do they handle the chores, their money, and their sex? How do they deal with former lovers, families, former wives, children, parents, and friends?

This lack of information prompted us to begin a descriptive research project interviewing male couples. That research has been published elsewhere (McWhirter and Mattison 1984). The study included interviews with 156 male couples who had been together for from 1 to more than 37 years. The interviews spanned a five-year period, and many couples were interviewed more than once, giving some longitudinal dimension to the results. One of the most important findings of our study was the discovery of stages in these relationships. We found that each new relationship forms a separate entity, much like a new child.

Although each of these relationships possesses its own unique qualities, nonetheless each one passes through a series of developmental stages with identifiable characteristics which tend to keep the men together. Many of the qualities of these stages are manifested by a balance between the positives and the negatives. More often than not, the negatives are viewed by each partner as flaws in the self or the other, when in reality they are merely some developmental issues of relationship growth. We like to compare this finding to the work of Benjamin Spock (1945) in which he popularized the findings of developmental psychologists' stages of childhood; rebellious, difficult-to-handle two-year-olds suddenly became manageable and acceptable because they had passed through a predictable stage labeled the *terrible twos*. With these findings a new saneness was introduced into childrearing by assigning characteristic behaviors and factors of physical growth to specific time periods or stages. The observations were not new to Spock's readers, the commonsense, easy-to-understand way he packaged the information simply normalized many of the changes of infancy that had previously been so anxiety provoking to parents. The same applies to the partners in a coupled relationship when they are distressed by issues that normally arise in one or the other stages of their relationship. Understanding that many of these issues are simply relationship stage–related rough spots in the road has and will provide great relief for the distress, anxiety, and depression that can all too often disrupt a male couple's life together. The discovery that the differences between them are not lethal to their relationship can provide the footing for problem solving.

Although this chapter is not about the study, it is intended as an introduction to the application of our staging theory to therapeutic issues with male couples. Therefore we are including a brief outline of stages and their characteristics, which can be found on the following page.

Stage One–Blending (Year One)
  Characteristics:
    1. Merging
    2. Limerence (see Note at end of chapter)
    3. Equalizing of partnership
    4. High sexual activity
Stage Two—Nesting (Years Two and Three)
  Characteristics:
    1. Homemaking
    2. Finding compatibility
    3. Decline of limerence
    4. Ambivalence
Stage Three—Maintaining (Years Four and Five)
  Characteristics:
    1. Reappearance of the individual
    2. Risk taking
    3. Dealing with conflict
    4. Establishing traditions
Stage Four—Building (Years Six Through Ten)
  Characteristics:
    1. Collaborating
    2. Increasing productivity
    3. Establishing independence
    4. Dependability of partner
Stage Five—Releasing (Years Eleven through Twenty)
  Characteristics:
    1. Trusting
    2. Merging of money and possessions
    3. Constriction
    4. Taking each other for granted
Stage Six—Renewing (Beyond Twenty Years)
  Characteristics:
    1. Achieving security
    2. Shifting perspective
    3. Restoring the partnership
    4. Remembering

Some Factors Affecting Staging

As with any developing entity, a relationship can be influenced and altered by many factors. Each partner brings a unique set of past experiences to the coupling. These can alter the way stages and characteristics form. For instance, couples with a wide disparity in ages, from a few years to as many as twenty years or more, may experience stages differently. Some of these couples pass through the early stages more quickly and smoothly, probably as a result of the older partner providing a degree of stability and guidance to the younger man.

Diversity of previous relationship experience can have positive and negative effects. Three or four previous painful experiences can slow down relationship stages, whereas past good ones can provide useful lessons for the facilitating of stages in the new pairing. Past marriages can have ramifications for staging, especially if the formerly married partner expects to pattern his new male-male relationship after heterosexual coupling.

Couples with widely different backgrounds, whether religious, ethnic, or socioeconomic, can bring very different values and expectations to the new relationship. Again, the effects can be positive or negative. Individual personality differences in the partners can also affect stage change by influencing the responses each man makes as his feelings change. This is especially true in how each individual deals with growing intimacy. Too much anxiety about it can retard the movement, and a great freedom to establish intimacy may move it onward more rapidly.

Stage discrepancy between partners is one of the most common influences on stage movement. When one partner moves more rapidly or more slowly through a stage than the other, stage development for the relationship is slowed. This is a problem we see so frequently in the clinic that the concept alone has been very useful in psychotherapy with gay couples. For instance, one partner may be individualizing, as in Stage Three, while the other partner is still deeply committed to the blending of Stage One.

Antihomosexual attitudes, which are discussed later in this

chapter, can have a deep influence on stages. The degree of individual homophobia can determine how quickly couples give themselves to the relationship or withhold from it. How much and how equally partners are out of the closet can assist or impede stage changes.

These are but a few of the influences affecting stages. They are not intended to form an exhaustive list, but rather an indication of how complex the concept really is. Although stages are organized around time periods and are presented in time-related linear sequence, there are many variations that include the stages and make them far more dynamic than our brief outline reveals. For instance, men who have had several previous relationships may shorten Stage One to a few weeks or months and move dramatically through Stage Two in a year. Some couples may linger longer in the warm glow of Stage One because of their similarities, while others with wide age differences may have many Stage Three characteristics after a few months or a year.

The movement from one stage to the next may appear to occur in an even, step-by-step, forward motion. In fact, most individuals and couples move a few steps back in the process of moving ahead. Also, many individuals do not traverse stages at the same speed at which their partner is traveling. Furthermore, individuals can be dealing with issues of more than one stage at once. Most importantly, each characteristic in every stage is a process, not an event. Dealing with stage-related issues happens over time, sometimes again and then again, and sometimes the process does not stop.

THE ASSESSMENT

Most therapists agree that the accurate assessment or diagnosis of the problem is critical to the process of treatment. Although the presenting condition in two different couples may be the same, the treatment for each may be very different based solely on the accuracy and adequacy of the diagnosis. As we began working with male couples, the paradigms used for diagnosis were all based on opposite-sex partnerships. The inaccuracies introduced into our diagnoses by the use of values and assumptions found among heterosexual couples accounted for many early failures. Just two examples of differences from heterosexual couples are: *(1)* among many male couples, the expectation of sexual exclusivity is nonexistent or diminishes rapidly after the first year, and *(2)* many couples maintain strict separation of money and possessions during the early years of their relationship. Couples and therapists themselves can even share old myths, such as that all male relationships are short-term or that gay men assume "butch-fem" roles within their partnerships. It is also essential for the diagnosis to evaluate the individual's and couple's antihomosexual attitudes. These can have profound effects upon their partnerships and are easily overlooked. It is easy to assume that gay men do not have antigay attitudes. However, in these couples, unrecognized homophobia and self-oppression can have subtle and grave consequences.

Diagnosis can be accomplished by a team composed of two males, by a male and female therapist, or by a single therapist of either sex. Experiences with all these combinations inclines us toward a single therapist, since studies in our clinic show the outcomes are about the same and a single therapist costs less. The diagnosis usually requires several sessions, including an initial session with the couple together. Seeing the couple together first helps to get the most valid understanding of the couple, since the partners tend to provide checks and balances as each tells his side of the story. After the introductory session together, each is seen individually to collect background and developmental histories. During this diagnostic phase we look for information in four major categories: *(1)* the nature of the presenting problem as seen by each partner and by the therapist; *(2)* the quality and the stage of the partners' relationship and other factors affecting stages; *(3)* the personality diagnosis for each partner, if there is one, and the principal mechanisms of defense for each; *(4)* the existence of other conditions, eg, antihomosexual attitudes, medical or health issues, and age differences. The following example illustrates the use of these diagnostic guidelines.

Jim is a 37-year-old business executive and Tom, his lover of eight years, is a 36 year old accountant. Jim is assertive and outgoing, belonging to business organizations and being active in public affairs, while Tom is a quiet, private person, content to focus all his energy on the relationship and their home. Jim has many friends and generally directs the couple's social life. In the six months prior to seeking therapy, Tom has been almost completely withdrawn from Jim, talking only when spoken to, staying home, having trouble sleeping and losing weight. Jim has two children from a marriage (boys aged 9 and 11); they spend two weekends each month with the male couple. The partners disagree about childrearing—Tom is lenient whereas Jim is firm. There has been a marked decline in their sexual contact in the past year. Tom says he is interested in meeting new friends, but Jim is afraid that Tom will find a new lover if that happens. Jim has frequent brief sexual encounters with others that Tom knows about. He becomes jealous but does not interfere. Tom says he is not ready for sex outside the relationship yet.

1. *Nature of presenting problem.*   It is different for each partner. Although both come to therapy with considerable unhappiness, each has a different laundry list of complaints. Tom wants more freedom within the relationship; he feels that Jim is too dominant and overpowering and that he uses a double standard. Tom also complains bitterly about the inadequacy of their sexual activity and is angry about Jim's outside contacts. Jim complains about Tom's passivity, withdrawal, and general lack of enthusiasm. Jim is also fearful of Tom's desire for greater freedom.

2. *Quality and stage of relationship.*   Although this couple has been together eight years and according to our theory should be in Stage Four, there appears to be considerable developmental discrepancy. Tom is struggling to individualize—a process common to Stage Three—while Jim has already individualized but does not want Tom to do the same. Tom's dependence on Jim is a problem for the couple.

3. *Individual personality and defenses.*   Tom is quiet and depressed. He uses avoidance, denial, and withdrawal as personality defenses. Jim is more assertive and demanding; he utilizes

rationalization and intellectualization. He also is unaware of his lover's depression.

4. *Homophobia.* There is considerable homophobia in Tom, and there is much difference in backgrounds, which creates some of the problems with their disagreements over how to rear the children.

This case shows how some of the problems are and can be stage-related while others are completely separate. Both types of problems are discussed in the sections that follow.

STAGE-RELATED PROBLEMS

Each of the stages has a unique set of problems. What follows is not intended to be a complete list of such problems, but rather some examples of common stage-related issues.

Not unexpectedly, one of the more common problems of Stage One is generated by the very intensity of the blending itself. The slightest sign of disagreement can precipitate anxiety and withdrawal from each other. The limerence of Stage One can also decline at different times for each partner and is always seen as a sign of loss of love between the two. "He doesn't love me any more," or "I don't love him like I used to." Breakups occur most often at the end of the first year when this decline in limerence is experienced. Some men seek limerence as an essential for any relationship and move from relationship to relationship when the limerence fades. We often refer to them as "limerence addicts." The fear of intimacy that is generated by the blending can also set the stage for problems. All too often, problems of intimacy in homosexual men are seen as part of the issue of orientation. Nothing could be further from the truth. Intimacy is a problem for all human beings, but most especially for men of any orientation. As a matter of fact, evidence points to the fact that intimacy may be easier for gay men than for their heterosexual fathers and brothers. We repeat, intimacy is a male problem, not a homosexual male problem. Looking for ways to equalize the giving and taking can also be problematic in this stage.

The major problems of Stage Two are seen with the decline in limerence and the invasion of the romance by the mundane. The partners see each other's faults and shortcomings, and most especially, the differences between them become exaggerated. We believe that finding compatibility is the single most important ingredient in keeping men together during the first decade of their relationships. The search for compatibility takes many forms: the insistence on compromise, the establishment of complementarity, and, sometimes, sacrifice. Helping two men explore their difficulties in establishing compatibility can be one of the most helpful things a therapist can do. Men do not think of the formation of their relationships in these terms, but it is easy to explain the concept to them for application in their own lives. The mixed feelings men develop during this stage—feelings that lead to the characteristic ambivalence we find here—need to be understood so that their negative effects can be minimized through cognitive awareness and universalization of the feelings and experience.

The reappearance of individuation in Stage Three can be the most threatening to a troubled relationship, especially if the merging of Stage One has been particularly intense and is still lingering for one or both partners. Partners often misinterpret the simple need for individualized time alone or with others as a negative signal. Conflicts arise as a result of the increasing risk taking. Outside sexual activity may begin or become more frequent, with jealousy and possessiveness making loud, unpleasant noises that are manifestations of anger and the anxiety that accompanies fear of loss or abandonment. This stage is a difficult one and a time when all couples could profit from some counseling assistance in navigating the more treacherous aspects of the course. Frequently, gay men are singled out for what is too often described as "promiscuity." As with intimacy, multiple sexual partners or promiscuity is not a gay man's issue, it is a man's issue, regardless of sexual orientation. It is just easier for two men, both with the same urges and drives to find each other than it is for a heterosexual man to find an equally desirous female partner.

Stage Four is the time of high output for male couples. The relationship takes a back seat, and this lack of attentiveness to it can be the major problem. Partners tend to drift apart as each establishes his independence. "Stage discrepancy," which will be discussed below, occurs most frequently in this stage. The results of working together so smoothly probably arises from the length of time in the relationship and the practice the partners have had doing things together. There is usually far less processing and discussion about each other during this period, which can produce problems.

In addition to problems related to the length of time in the relationship, such as boredom, couples in Stage Five have the burden of concerns accompanying the process of aging. Routine and monotony can become the enemy. The tendency for each partner to become more fixed and rigid in personality characteristics while struggling to change the other can also plague men who have been together for 10 years or longer. The single most important characteristic that keeps men together and seemingly happy after 10 years together is lack of possessiveness. When partners continue to cling to each other or continue to try to change each other, this stage can become a very unpleasant period.

Couples in Stage Six often continue to have the problems of Stage Five, but with the increase in age and the attainment of goals there is restlessness and sometimes withdrawal and feelings of aimlessness. Sometimes these couples begin having arguments— they irritate each other with greater frequency. We found more antihomosexual attitudes in these couples, but we hesitate to call them stage related in general, since many of these poisonous attitudes were instilled in these men long before being gay was accepted more positively.

Therapists will find other stage related problems among couples they are treating. The few listed above are only the tip of the iceberg, so to speak. The concept of staging, however, is useful for all couples.

STAGE DISCREPANCY

More often than not, couples do not progress through the stages simultaneously. If there is a wide difference in the process, problems arise that we have identified as "stage discrepancies." It is very common to find couples together seven or eight years with one partner in an individualized, comfortable position (Stage Four) and the other still dependent and clinging (Stage Two or Three). In clinical practice, regardless of the presenting problems, we find more than half the couples seen in our Institute are laboring with some degree of stage discrepancy. Couples experience considerable relief when this concept is explained to them, just as a man with chest pain is relieved when the physician informs him it is only muscle strain, not a heart attack.

When couples understand the concept of stage discrepancy, they realize that their problems are not flaws in themselves or their partnerships but correctable, temporary, developmental differences in the growth of their relationships. Although all discrepancies may not lend themselves to rapid adjustment, the understanding derived from the cognitive framework of stage discrepancy makes the affective problems easier to handle and to treat. After all, when a man with chest pain knows the exercise will not injure his heart, running need no longer be anxiety provoking (McWhirter and Mattison 1982).

NON-STAGE-RELATED PROBLEMS

Personality differences and the ways each individual deals with anxiety, fear, guilt, trust, and intimacy can cause problems as in any dyadic relationship. There are, however, some problems that are unique to male couples; many of them also apply to female couples, but in this chapter we are limiting our observations to gay men.

Antihomosexual Attitudes

The pervasiveness of antihomosexual attitudes touches every person but affects gay people profoundly. These attitudes include *(1)* ignorance, *(2)* prejudice, *(3)* oppression, and *(4)* homophobia. All together, or in some combination, they are overtly or covertly present in every male couple we have ever seen. Many men have been able to understand and minimize their influence, but most have not completely recognized the depth of their own homophobia or the degree of their own self-oppression. A careful diagnosis and differentiation among the four attitudes is important as the couple's therapy begins.

Of these four antihomosexual attitudes, homophobia is the most insidious and difficult to identify and treat. A diagnosis of homophobia is confirmed by ruling out the other antihomosexual attitudes. Ignorance is changed by knowledge. We use extensive reading of books and articles, the viewing of video tapes, attendance at lectures, and other sources of accurate information to dispel the partners' lack of knowledge. It requires more than new knowledge to change prejudice. There must be some accompanying impactful positive emotional experience, such as can occur with a group. Oppression, especially self-oppression, may take the form of unwitting assumptions about the negative attitudes of others toward homosexual persons. Homophobia is recognized by its persistence in the face of knowledge and the reduction of prejudice. The continued presence of low self-esteem and lack of self-acceptance, resistance to coming out, and the continued rejection of some aspects of homosexuality are evidence of homophobia's virulence. The clinician must be alert and evaluate the extensive hidden manifestations of these antihomosexual attitudes (McWhirter and Mattison 1982).

Levels of Being Out of the Closet

The degree to which partners are open about their homosexuality can be an important ingredient in relationship stability. We have seen highly closeted couples together for 30 years or more. We sometimes feel that these couples' shared "closetedness" contributes to the togetherness of their relationships. On the other hand, we also find that the closet can be the worst enemy for some relationships and for many individuals. It is very important to determine the individual's and the couple's level of openness when doing an evaluation. For example, one partner may be fully out to his entire family, and the other may not be. One may be active in gay politics, the other a frightened and closeted elementary school teacher. These differences can wreak havoc with a relationship.

Absence of Role Models

Gay male couples usually have no reliable relationship role models to pattern themselves after or, indeed, to avoid patterning themselves after. Those couples who try to follow the traditional heterosexual models of marriage invariably find themselves unable to survive the rigidities imposed by the usual gender-related expectations. Male couples do not function as husband and wife with one assuming one role and the other the other. We began our research with male couples precisely because our patients were asking us questions about male couple role models for which we had no answers. Gradually some models are evolving in our literature and theater, but all too often even these models are following old stereotypes of the "butch-fem" genre.

Communications

For most heterosexual couples seeking therapy, a lack of communication is a major problem. Gay men do encounter communication difficulties, especially at later stages in their relationships, but more often male couples have a tendency to overcommunicate, processing their feelings and thoughts interminably without progress, causing relationship fatigue and distress.

Other Causes

Socioeconomics, family backgrounds, levels of education, religion, values, previous relationships, illness, financial setbacks, individual emotional problems, sexual dysfunctions, and jealousy are examples of other sources of conflict that are not related to stages or to sexual orientation.

Regardless of the cause, couples seeking therapy manifest their distress in a limited number of ways, including anger and hostility, withdrawal and depression, increased anxiety, fear, or some other form of unhappiness. Identification of the problem and its probable causes, achieved through adequate diagnosis, is the key to the choice of therapy and its ultimate effectiveness in improving the quality of life for those seeking assistance.

CHOICE OF THERAPY

In addition to evaluating the problem and its roots, the therapist should ask the couple about their needs and expectations. The therapeutic approach must be tailored to the individual couple. For those with stage-related problems, a short-term counseling approach that may include explanations, reading, and a few group sessions with other couples in similar circumstances can send them on their way with renewed confidence. If the diagnostic workup exposes depression, anxiety, or fear in one partner or the other, a move toward individual dynamically oriented therapy is indicated and recommended for one partner only; however, we continue to see the couple together at intervals to include the other partner in the treatment process. Some couples have stage discrepancies based on personality characteristics of a partner. These couples require a marital therapy approach with emphasis on their interactional dynamics. Marital therapy is also useful for couples with conflicts unrelated to sexual orientation or the stages of their relationship. For example, jealousy or differences in values and expectations are common. Male couples share many of the problems seen in any dyadic relationship. For couples with sexual dysfunctions, the choice of sex therapy may be specific or adjunctive to marital therapy, depending upon the results of the diagnosis (McWhirter and Mattison 1978, 1980). Crisis intervention for couples in acute distress requires more rapid diagnosis with very directive short-term (two or three sessions) treatment focused on the specific causes of the crisis. Group therapy for couples can be particularly effective when socialization, problem-solving, and sharpening of communication skills are major therapeutic goals. Diagnosis may indicate no need for psychotherapy per se, but rather a need for education and information accompanied by social activities with other gay men and women. Social, academic, and recreational groups and clubs for gay people are valuable tools here.

THE THERAPIST

We do not believe there is a specific form of therapy for male couples. However, possessing some knowledge about their relationship stages can be extremely useful for any therapist working with them, regardless of his or her therapeutic training. Nevertheless, the therapist who treats homosexual persons must possess certain attitudes and levels of knowledge in order to be minimally competent on the job. We believe that therapists need to know about their own antihomosexual attitudes, especially their own homophobia and how it affects them and their patients. Therapists working with male couples must also see these relationships as viable and desirable life-styles in general, if not necessarily for each and every couple seeking help. Therapists who believe that homosexuality represents a distinct psychopathological condition in itself are encouraged to refer male couples to colleagues who do not share that belief.

CONCLUSION

The application of relationship staging theory to male couples has already proved itself a valuable addition to our therapeutic armamentarium. Understanding some of the inner dynamics that seem to occur in various degrees in all male couples leads us to more effective diagnoses which in turn help identify more effective treatment methods. This theory of relationship stages is new and needs further field testing of usefulness in the hands of other therapists. There may be characteristics other than those we have identified, the time frames may vary, and there may be more stages. We can learn about these if we listen attentively to our patients, because it is they who will teach us the most about their relationships.

NOTE: In *Love and Limerence* (1979), Dorothy Tennov introduces the word "limerence" to describe the state of falling in love or being romantically in love. Tennov describes the basic components of limerence, which include *(1)* intrusive thinking about the desired person (who is the limerent object); *(2)* acute longing for reciprocation of feelings and thoughts; *(3)* buoyancy (a feeling of walking on air) when reciprocation seems evident; *(4)* a general intensity of feelings that leaves other concerns in the background; and *(5)* emphasizing the other's positive attributes and avoiding the negative (or rendering them, at least emotionally, into positive attributes). Tennov includes sexual attraction as an essential component of limerence, but admits exceptions. Sexual attraction alone, however, is not enough to denote true limerence.

References

McWhirter DP, Mattison AM: The treatment of sexual dysfunctions in gay male couples. J Sex Marital Ther 4:213–218, 1978

McWhirter DP, Mattison AM: Treatment of sexual dysfunctions in homosexual male couples, in Principles and Practices of Sex Therapy. Edited by Leiblum SR, Pervin LA. New York, The Guildford Press, 1980

McWhirter DP, Mattison AM: Psychotherapy for gay male couples, in Homosexuality and Psychotherapy. Edited by Gorsiorek J. New York, Haworth Press, 1982

McWhirter DP, Mattison AM: The Male Couple. Englewood Cliffs, NJ, Prentice-Hall, 1984

Saghir MT, Robins T: Male and Female Homosexuality: A Comprehensive Investigation. Baltimore, Williams & Wilkins Co, 1973

Spock B: Baby and Child Care. New York, Simon and Schuster, 1945

Tennov D: Love and Limerence. New York, Stein & Day, 1979